History of the Cavalry
of the Army of
the Potomac

History of the Cavalry
of the Army of
the Potomac

Including Pope's Army of Virginia and
the Cavalry Operations in West Virginia
During the American Civil War

Charles D. Rhodes

LEONAUR

History of the Cavalry of the Army of the Potomac: Including Pope's Army of Virginia and the Cavalry Operations in West Virginia During the American Civil War
by Charles D. Rhodes

Originally published under the title
History of the Cavalry of the Army of the Potomac Including that of the Army of Virginia (Pope's), and also the History of the Operations of the Federal Cavalry in West Virginia During the War

Published by Leonaur Ltd

ISBN: 978-1-84677-506-2 (hardcover)
ISBN: 978-1-84677-505-5 (softcover)

http://www.leonaur.com

Publisher's Notes

The opinions expressed in this book are those of the author and are not necessarily those of the publisher.

Contents

Introduction

The preparation of the following pages, especially that portion dealing with the events of the first two years of the war, has not been easy. To evolve a general history from those of individuals, and yet not deal with any one regiment to the prejudice of others; to separate the operations of the cavalry from those of the other arms, and yet preserve that degree of relationship which a part bears to the whole; to touch upon the details of the battle and the march, and yet not transgress the prescribed limits of this little history— all these have been difficulties which have severally and collectively taxed the writer's resources to the utmost. The almost total absence of works of reference, except histories of individual regiments and the official records of the War of the Rebellion, has in itself involved a vast deal of labour. It is, perhaps, not too much to say that a history of the cavalry of the Army of the Potomac might very easily have filled three times as many pages as have here been devoted to it; and the writer has, much against his will, been compelled to cut out matter of the greatest interest At the same time, while he has borne in mind that this history is intended to be a faithful chronicle of the life of the Federal cavalry, he has tried not to lose sight of the fact that a mere record of events is certain to be monotonous reading.

CHAPTER 1

Formation to Chickahominy Bridge

At the breaking out of the War of the Rebellion the cavalry force at the disposal of the United States

Government consisted of the First and Second Regiments of Dragoons, one regiment of Mounted Rifles, and the First and Second Regiments of Cavalry. When President Lincoln issued his call for three-months volunteers, another regiment, the Sixth, was added to the five others, but, for the time, this was the extent of the increase in the cavalry. Volunteer infantry and artillery poured into Washington from all parts of the North, but volunteer cavalry neither came nor were encouraged to come. Absurd as it now appears, it was the intention of the Federal authorities to confine the cavalry to the six regular regiments. The North confidently expected to crush the Rebellion at once. Cavalry was an expensive arm, and experienced officers knew that years were required to produce an efficient trooper. Even such a veteran as General Scott gave it as his opinion that, owing to the broken and wooded character of the field of operations and the improvements in rifled firearms, the role of the cavalry would be unimportant and secondary. McClellan's report of the preliminary operations in West Virginia says:

"Cavalry was absolutely refused, but the governors of

the States complied with my request and organized a few companies, which were finally mustered into the United States service and proved very useful."

Only seven companies of cavalry took part in the battle of Bull Run, but the firm front which they displayed while covering the precipitate retreat of the Federal army probably saved a large proportion of the army from annihilation by Stuart's cavalry, and has never received the recognition which it deserved.

On the 27th of July, 1861, McClellan assumed command of what was destined to be called the Army of the Potomac, and the regular cavalry regiments were reorganized, and renumbered consecutively from "one" to "six."

With the organization of the Army of the Potomac begins the real history of its cavalry, but for two long years until its reorganization under Hooker— its history is one of neglect, disorganization, and misuse. McClellan's one idea of the shortcomings of the cavalry was that it was not large enough. Meanwhile it furnished guides, orderlies, and grooms for staff officers, and was so divided up among corps, division, and brigade commanders as to completely subvert its true value, bringing sarcasm and ignominy on what should have been one of the most powerful factors in the overthrow of the Rebellion.

The drill regulations of the cavalry at the breaking out of the war called at that time "tactics"— were modified from those of the French dragoons, and had been found unsuited to the needs of cavalry operating in the United States. General Philip St. G. Cooke had accordingly prepared a new system, which was approved by the War Department in October, 1861, but did not come into use on account of the conditions which obtained at the time. This, without doubt, proved a great restriction upon the usefulness of the arm.

The armament of the volunteer regiments, which were mustered in with some show of interest after the disaster at Bull Run, were along the same lines as that of the regular regiments of that day, and was in charge of General Stoneman. Though suffering from a deficiency in cavalry arms and equipments, every cavalry soldier was armed with a sabre and revolver as soon as circumstances permitted, and at least two squadrons in every regiment were armed with carbines.

One volunteer regiment, the Sixth Pennsylvania Cavalry (Rush's Lancers), was armed with the lance, in addition to the pistol, twelve carbines being afterwards added to the equipment of each company, for picket and scouting duties. The lances were carried from December, 1861, until May, 1863, when they were discarded for the carbine, as being ill-adapted for use in the wooded country through which the command operated.

The carbines issued were of various patterns, generally the Sharpe's, until the advent of the Spencer in 1863. The revolver was the Colt's. The saddle was the McClellan, and, with the remaining horse equipments, had been adopted through recommendations made by General McClellan after his official European tour in 1860. The saddle, however, was covered with rawhide instead of leather, and became very uncomfortable when split.

The original regulations governing the mustering in of volunteer regiments required the cavalry to furnish their own horses as well as horse equipments;[1] but this was later modified, and the Government furnished them, as they had done to the regular regiments. But the horses furnished were in most cases very poor animals, due to fraud on the part of Government contractors, and the overtaxed resources of the Quartermaster's Department.

---

1. See Appendix 1.

On the 15th of October, 1861, the organization of the cavalry consisted of a small brigade under General Stoneman, and some eleven or twelve other regiments, attached to divisions of infantry.[2] Its strength, November 12th, aggregated 8,125, of which but 4,753 are reported as "present for duty, equipped." It was constantly drilled during the fall and winter, with enough scouting and outpost duty in the Virginia hills to give the cavalry regiments a foretaste of actual service. And just preceding the Peninsular campaign, General Stoneman with a brigade made a reconnaissance along the Orange & Alexandria Railroad as far as Cedar Run.

In March, 1862, the Peninsular Army was transported southward, and the siege of Yorktown was begun. The cavalry reserve, which was under that veteran cavalryman, General P. St. G. Cooke, was organized as two brigades under Generals Emory and Blake, and consisted of six regiments.[3] The rest of the cavalry was divided up among the army corps and the various headquarters. Every available hour spared from outpost duty was still utilized for drill, and when the enemy abandoned his lines at Yorktown, the cavalry was called upon to pursue.

General Cooke encountered the enemy in force at Fort Magruder, but as he failed to be supported by Hooker's Division through causes which have become historic, he was obliged to fall back. But not before the First U. S. Cavalry had made two brilliant charges, capturing a regimental standard. Major Williams four squadrons of the Sixth U. S. Cavalry, which was cut off by a large force of the enemy, saved itself by promptly wheeling about by fours and charging the pursuers.

Had there been a larger force of Federal cavalry, or had

---

2. See Appendix 2.

3. Emory's Brigade: Fifth U. S. Cavalry, Sixth U. S. Cavalry, Sixth Pennsylvania Cavalry. Blake's Brigade: First U. S. Cavalry, Eighth Pennsylvania Cavalry, Barker's squadron Illinois Cavalry.

it been properly supported by the infantry divisions, it is probable that the battle of Williamsburg, which followed, would never have been fought. Longstreet had not intended to fight here, but finding his rear guard successful and posted in a strong position, and a large portion of his force involved, he gave battle.

The cavalry took little part in this battle. Williamsburg was abandoned by the enemy on the 6th, and Colonel Averell, with portions of the Third Pennsylvania and Eighth Illinois Cavalry, pressed on in pursuit as far as New Kent, recovering five pieces of artillery and capturing twenty-one prisoners.

"From this time on," as a distinguished cavalry officer has said, "affairs with the cavalry, through no fault of its own, went from bad to worse. Detachments from its strength were constantly increased, and it was hampered by instructions which crippled it for all useful action." But in spite of the disadvantages under which it laboured, it displayed the same brave devotion to duty which was afterwards to be put to such good account during the last two years of the war.

During the next few days, the cavalry was almost constantly engaged in reconnaissance duty, and although there were numerous minor skirmishes, nothing of importance occurred until the taking of Hanover Court House (May 27-29), when the Fifth and Sixth United States Cavalry, supported by the Seventeenth New York Infantry, cut off and captured the greater part of an entire regiment the Twenty-eighth North Carolina Infantry continuing the pursuit two and one-half miles beyond the town.

In pursuance of the general plan of cutting the enemy's communications with northern Virginia, cavalry brigades under General Emory and Colonel Warren destroyed the bridges over the South Anna and Pamunkey rivers, and engaged in many creditable skirmishes with the enemy. Some of the volunteer cavalry, during these operations, were under fire for the first time.

The cavalry's part in the battle of Fair Oaks (May 29th) was insignificant. Nothing else could be expected, considering its disunited condition and anomalous status; so that when, two weeks later (June 13th), Stuart, with about 1,200 cavalry, passed completely around the Federal army and fell on the weak right flank of the cavalry, there could be but one result. The cavalry was blamed for not having given notice of Stuart's approach; and when General Cooke, with a small cavalry force, was tacked on to an infantry division and told to catch Stuart, his failure to strike his swift-moving adversary was criticised in these words: "I have seen no energy or spirit in the pursuit by General Cooke of the enemy, nor has he exhibited the characteristics of a skillful and active guardian of our flanks."[4]

Time has shown that General Cooke received positive orders from the commanding general of the left wing to regulate his pursuit by the march of the infantry column, and on no account to precede it. "The officer of today, even though he has had no experience in war, with the record of cavalry marches before him, can imagine the effect of such an order on a dashing, chivalrous, enthusiastic cavalry officer, chafing under the restraints that had already been placed upon him by a soldier who had learned from the books that a forced march for cavalry for one day was twenty-five miles."[5]

In the passage of the Army of the Potomac over the Chickahominy, General Porter, with the Fifth Army Corps, was charged with covering the movement and keeping the enemy in check. All the cavalry was placed under his orders, and the battle of Gaines Mill, which followed (June

---

4. Report of General Fitz John Porter.
5. General Merritt, in *Journal U. 8. Cavalry Association,* June, 1895.

27th), is remarkable for the stubborn resistance of the cavalry under General Cooke.[6]

The line of battle formed the arc of a circle, almost parallel to the Chickahominy, and Cooke's division, consisting of two small brigades, was placed behind the breaks of a plateau, in rear of the extreme left of the line. During the day the Confederate army, reinforced by the army of Stonewall Jackson from northern Virginia, made four desperate assaults on the Union lines, and every available infantryman was brought into action. In rear of the left of the line there was not a single reserve, save the cavalry and considerable artillery. The day was fast drawing to a close, when the Confederates made a final effort to force the left flank and cut it off from the bridge over the Chickahominy. The centre and left of the line gave way under overwhelming numbers, many of the regiments being completely demoralized. The reserve artillery, left without support, had begun to limber up, when, by order of General Cooke, they were ordered to maintain their position, and were assured that the cavalry would support them. The artillery willingly complied and opened a heavy fire on the advancing infantry lines. When almost too close for an effective charge, General Cooke ordered Captain Whiting, commanding the Fifth U. S. Cavalry, to charge with his regiment. Numbering but 220 sabres, the little force moved out under a heavy fire, and a portion of the line struck the enemy intact, and were only stopped by the woods at the bottom of the slope. The casualties in the charge were fifty-eight, with twenty-four horses killed, a sacrifice that was well worth the results attained. Under cover of the charge the artillery was safely withdrawn, its bold stand having delayed the enemy's advance long enough for the re-forming of the best disciplined infantry regiments.

6. See Appendix 3.

Had this determined stand not been made, the seizure of the Chickahominy bridge and the capture of at least a portion of Porter's command would undoubtedly have followed. And yet General Porter reported that the cavalry caused the loss of the action. The Comte de Paris, in a letter to General Cooke, February 2, 1877, has said: "The sacrifice of some of the bravest of the cavalry certainly saved a part of the artillery, as did, on a larger scale, the Austrian cavalry on the evening of Sadowa. The main fact is that with your cavalry you did all that cavalry could do to stop the rout."[7]

Not a more glorious act occurred during the entire war than this misrepresented charge of the Fifth U. S. Cavalry, as a sacrifice for the withdrawal of the artillery. The survivors should have been decorated, and, had they belonged to a French or German army, they would undoubtedly have been thus rewarded.

About June 24th General Stoneman was placed in command of all the cavalry on the right of the army (about 2,000 in all), and was charged with picketing the country towards Hanover Court House. During the Seven Days battles he was guarding the region from the Meadow Bridge to the Pamunkey, with the Seventeenth New York Infantry and Eighteenth Massachusetts in support. The manoeuvring of the enemy was such as to cut off Stoneman's command from Porter's corps, and, after falling back on White House, where he destroyed immense quantities of stores to prevent their falling into the enemy's hands, he retreated to Yorktown, arriving there the 29th instant. These cavalry regiments attached to the army corps during this movement performed arduous and pains taking duties.

By an order published July 8, 1862, part of the volunteer cavalry of the Army of the Potomac was organized by General Stoneman into two brigades, commanded by Colonels

---

7. *Battles and Leaders of the Civil War* Vol. 2., page 344.

Averell and Gregg.[8] To Averell was assigned the task of thoroughly patrolling the country in front of the right wing and flank, and to Colonel Gregg was given similar duties on the left flank. Diminutive as this force was for the many duties it was called upon to perform, it performed them well. But again was the cavalry called upon to furnish guides scouts, orderlies, and escorts, until the regiments dwindle down to mere nothings. In fact, as General Merritt has said, "After Gaines Mill, the cavalry of the Army of the Potomac had no history of which it had reason to be proud, until the reorganization of the army, with Hooker in command."

---

8. First Brigade (Averell's): Third Pennsylvania, First New York, Fourth Pennsylvania, Cavalry. Second Brigade (1, Gregg's; 2, Pleasanton's): Eighth Illinois, Eighth Pennsylvania, Sixth New York. To Sumner's corps, Barker's squadron. To Heintzelman's corps, Delaney's squadron, Fifth Pennsylvania Cavalry. To Keyes' corps, one squadron, Eighth Illinois Cavalry. To Porter's corps, one squadron, First New York Cavalry. To Franklin's corps, one squadron, First New York Cavalry.

CHAPTER 2

The Army of Virginia to Bull Run

On the 26th of June General John Pope had been assigned to the command of the Army of Virginia, composed
of the commands of Generals Banks, Fremont, and Mc-
Dowell. Fremont had succeeded Rosecrans in command
of the Mountain Department, March 29th, but under his
administration and those of his predecessors, the Federal
cavalry in West Virginia had performed no conspicuous
deeds. The country was ill-suited for manoeuvring large
bodies of cavalry; but for scouting and reconnoitering small
bodies could be made very useful, as shown by the value to
McClellan of the hybrid commands known as McMullen's
Rangers, the Ringgold Cavalry, and Burdsall's Cavalry. In
fact, partisan warfare was a distinct feature of the operations
in West Virginia throughout the war.

A year after the beginning of the war, the Mountain
Department, which included West Virginia, contained thir-
ty-six companies of cavalry, aggregating 2,741 men; but
they were poorly equipped and mounted many of them
dismounted. And these, with the insufficient infantry and
artillery forces, guarded a frontier 350 miles long, 300 miles
of railroad, and 200 miles of water communication.

In his report of the battle of Kernstown (March 23, 1862),
one of the bright spots in the successive misfortunes of the

Union forces in the Shenandoah Valley, General Shields says: "My cavalry is very ineffective. If I had one regiment of excellent cavalry, armed with carbines, I could have doubled the enemy's loss."

The cavalry which Fremont brought to the Army of Virginia were partly dismounted, and the horses of those who were mounted were in a great measure so broken down and starved as to be well-nigh useless. The mounted forces of Banks and McDowell were in much the same miserable condition. The consolidated morning report of July 31, 1862, shows that out of 8,738 cavalry in the three corps, 3,000 are deducted as "unfit for service." Such a proportion is a commentary on the condition of the cavalry of the Army of Virginia at this time.

And yet this little force did excellent service; partly, perhaps, through the efficiency of those who commanded it, but principally on account of its wise use by the commanding general.

Pope's general instructions directed him to cover Washington, and pending the transfer of McClellan's troops from Harrison's Landing to Aquia Creek, Va., he was charged with resisting at all hazard any possible advance of the enemy.

Accordingly General King, at Fredericksburg, was directed to send out detachments of his cavalry to operate on the line of the Virginia Central Railroad and destroy communications between Richmond and the Shenandoah. The cavalry expeditions sent out were highly successful.

At the same time Banks was directed to push all his cavalry towards Gordonsville, and its execution was entrusted to General John I. Hatch, an officer of the regular cavalry. But this officer, instead of pushing forward with all haste, burdened himself with infantry, artillery, and wagon trains, so that when Pope supposed the bridges and railroad destroyed in the vicinity of Charlottesville and Gordonsville,

Hatch's command had just reached Madison Court House. This movement illustrates the common idea of the use of cavalry at this period. Hatch's delay allowed Jackson s advance to occupy Gordonsville. and the movements contemplated became impracticable. Hatch was relieved from command, and was succeeded by Buford, as chief of cavalry of Banks' corps.

On August 7th the cavalry of the Army of Virginia was distributed as follows: Buford's brigade, at Madison Court House, picketing the Rapidan from Barnett's Ford to the Blue Ridge; Bayard's brigade at Rapidan Station, picketing from Barnett's to Raccoon Fords. (Buford and Bayard were young officers of the regular cavalry.) Pickets were also established from Raccoon Ford to the forks of the Rappahannock. The whole disposition of the cavalry was admirably arranged as a screening force, and on August 7th and 8th performed valuable service in retarding Jackson's advance and keeping Pope informed of the enemy's movements.

At the battle of Cedar Mountain,[1] which occurred the following day, the cavalry fell slowly back as the enemy advanced, and rendered effective service throughout the day, a squadron of the First Pennsylvania Cavalry making a most gallant charge against a body of the enemy which was about to charge the Union batteries. The squadron lost an aggregate of 93 men out of the 164 who participated in the charge.

As Jackson fell back across the Rapidan, the cavalry kept touch with him, and reoccupied their old picket line, stretching from Raccoon Ford to the base of the Blue Ridge. Reconnaissances, too, were pushed forward, and a cavalry command sent out on August 16th captured General Stuart's adjutant-general with important dispatches, the tenor of which strongly influenced Pope in his deci-

1. See Appendix 4.

sion to fall back across the Rappahannock, which he did August 17th and 18th.

At this time the cavalry was greatly fatigued. Pope says: "Our cavalry numbered on paper about 4,000 men, but their horses were completely broken down, and there were not 500 men capable of doing as much service as should be expected from cavalry." That the cavalry would play an unimportant part in the subsequent movements leading up to and culminating in the battle of Bull Run would be expected from their miserable condition. With broken-down horses it was impossible to cover the front of the army, or to make reconnaissances. Speaking of the condition of the cavalry on the morning of the battle of Bull Run, Pope says: "The artillery and cavalry horses had been in harness and saddled continually for ten days, and had had no forage for two days previous." But the services of the cavalry under their two efficient brigade commanders could not receive greater praise than when General Pope says: "Generals Bayard and Buford commanded the cavalry belonging to the Army of Virginia. Their duties were peculiarly arduous and hazardous, and it is not too much to say that throughout the operations, from the first to the last day of the campaign, scarcely a day passed that these officers did not render service which entitles them to the gratitude of the Government."[2]

Thus did the cavalry acquit itself. It had not always been used wisely, nor was it kept supplied with remounts and forage as it should have been. Efficiency, which comes only with experience, was gradually gaining ground in spite of many obstacles. The true worth of cavalry, and consequently its true employment, was beginning to be better comprehended. An order issued by General Pope, soon after the battle of Cedar Mountain, directing the cavalry de-

2. See Appendix 5.

tachments at brigade and division headquarters to report for duty to their chiefs of cavalry, and greatly reducing the number of orderlies, marks a decided change in the condition of the cavalry; but the time was still far distant when it was to be given a status in keeping with its importance, and when it was able to vindicate itself in the eyes of those who "never saw a dead cavalryman."

CHAPTER 3

Antietam to Fredericksburg

On the 5th day of September, 1862, the Army of the Potomac and the Army of Virginia were consolidated, and General McClellan assumed command of both armies.

Contrary to public expectation, General Lee invaded Maryland instead of attacking Washington, and the Army of the Potomac, while shielding the national capital, endeavoured to keep touch with the army of invasion. Had McClellan had at his disposal at this time an adequate cavalry force, his task would have been made infinitely more simple.

But the cavalry, especially that portion which had passed through Pope's campaign, was in deplorable condition for aggressive action. Pleasanton's cavalry division, weakened though it was by its experience on the Peninsula, was best able to take the field, and early in September was reconnoitering the fords of the Potomac. On the 9th it occupied Barnesville, and captured the battle-flag of the Twelfth Virginia Cavalry. On the 13th the right wing and centre of the Federal army having reached Frederick, the cavalry cleared the passage over the Catoctin Hills, and early on the morning of the 14th found the enemy occupying advantageous positions at South Mountain, on either side of the gap through which the National Road passed.

The enemy was routed from his positions by the Federal

army, but the cavalry took little part in the battle. Pleasanton deployed a portion of his cavalry dismounted during the day, causing the enemy to mass a considerable force on the right of the Confederate position.

Lee's army withdrew so as to cover the Shepherdstown Ford of the Potomac, and the cavalry, followed by three army corps, pursued by way of Boonesborough. At the latter place the cavalry caught up with the enemy's rear guard, and, charging repeatedly, drove the enemy two miles beyond the town. The enemy left 30 dead and 50 wounded upon the field, besides 2 pieces of artillery and 250 prisoners captured; while the loss to the Union cavalry was but 1 killed and 15 wounded.

On the 17th, the date of the battle of Antietam, the cavalry moved to Antietam Bridge, which was found to be under a cross-fire of the enemy's artillery. Cavalry skirmishers were thrown forward, and, aided by the horse batteries of the division, the enemy's batteries were driven from their positions. The main battle was between the infantry and artillery of both armies, and resulted in the withdrawal of Lee's army into Virginia.

On the 18th the cavalry was feeling the enemy and collecting stragglers; on the 19th, pushing the enemy's rear guard at the fords of the Potomac; and thereafter, for some time, it was so disposed as to cover the principal fords, making frequent reconnaissances into Virginia to develop the enemy's position and movements.

For these duties the strength of the cavalry was found to be inadequate. Overwork and disease had broken down the horses to such an extent that when on October 11th General Stuart made a raid into Pennsylvania with 2.000 men, McClellan could mount but 800 men to follow him.[3]

3. *Rebellion Records,* Vol. 19., Part 1., page 71. For strength, "present and absent," see Appendix 7.

To meet this raid, Averell — then on the upper Potomac — moved down the north side of the river, while Pleasanton, taking the Cavestown — Mechanicstown road, was disposed to cut off the raiding force should it cross by any of the fords below the main army. Upon arriving at Mechanicstown, Pleasanton learned that the enemy was but an hour ahead of him retreating towards the mouth of the Monocacy; and, although his own force numbered about one-fourth that of the enemy, he pursued vigorously,[4] and attacked Stuart's rear guard with such energy that the latter was prevented from crossing the Monocacy Ford, and was forced to move to White's Ford, three miles below. Had the latter ford been occupied by troops as was originally ordered, it is quite probable that Stuart would have been captured or badly crippled. A larger cavalry force, or even a supply of serviceable horses for the Army of the Potomac, might have prevented this raid, which had the effect of drawing a considerable force from Lee's tired army, produced great consternation among the people of the North, and led to the loss of much property.

On September 10th General Buford had been announced as chief-of-cavalry of the Army of the Potomac, but the office was simply a staff position, and was attended with very little, if any, independence of action. So far as the cavalry was concerned, the chief-of-cavalry was the executive officer of the commanding general.

On October 1st General Bayard was assigned to the command of all the cavalry about Washington, south of the Potomac; and on the 21st General Pleasanton was given a cavalry brigade, consisting of the Sixth U. S. Cavalry, the Eighth Pennsylvania, the Eighth Illinois, the Third Indiana, and the Eighth New York Cavalry regiments.

On the 26th Pleasanton crossed the Potomac at Berlin,

4. Pleasanton marched seventy-eight miles in twenty-four hours.

and during the next few days was employed, as was also the brigade of Bayard, in gaining information of the enemy's movements, resulting in skirmishes at Snicker's Gap, Upperville, Aldie, Mountville, Philomont, and Manassas Gap. On November 5th his brigade fought an action at Barbee's Cross-Roads, with Stuart's command of about 3,000 cavalry, accompanied by four pieces of artillery. Gregg, with the Eighth Pennsylvania and the Sixth United States, turned the enemy's right; Davis, with the Eighth New York, attacked the left; and Farnsworth, with the Eighth Illinois, moved against the centre. During the engagement, Davis was met by a much superior force, about to charge him. He quickly overcame the disproportion in numbers by dismounting several of his companies behind a stone wall, and their galling front and flank fire soon threw the enemy into confusion. This accomplished, Davis, with the remainder of the regiment, mounted, charged, routed the enemy, and drove him from the field. The Confederates left thirty-seven dead upon the field, while the Union loss was but five killed and eight wounded. This manoeuvre of fighting dismounted behind obstacles with a portion of a command, and charging the enemy in the flank with the remainder mounted, became a very common and effective method of fighting throughout the war.

On November 7th General McClellan was superseded as commander of the Army of the Potomac by General Burnside, and the army was organized into three grand divisions the right, centre, and left, commanded by Sumner, Hooker, and Franklin. An order of the 21st instant assigned the cavalry divisions of Pleasanton, Bayard, and Averell to the three grand divisions respectively.

Burnside moved his army down the north side of the Rappahannock on November 15th, and reached Falmouth on the 20th. Although the river was fordable a few miles above the town, and Lee's army had not yet reached Falmouth at this date, Burnside did not cross the river until the 11th of December. The passage of the river was effected without much opposition, but in the subsequent attempts to turn the enemy's position on the heights in rear of Fredericksburg, the Federal army was obliged to fall back. Both armies remained in position until the night of December 10th, when General Burnside withdrew his forces to the north bank of the Rappahannock.

During the advance along the north bank of the river, begun on November 15th, the cavalry was in rear, employed in covering the fords, and this duty gave rise to much skirmishing. On November 16th at the United States Ford, and on the 28th at Hartwood Church, Bayard's and Averell's cavalry divisions were engaged ; and on the 28th to 30th of the month the brigade attached to the reserve grand division, whose headquarters were near Fairfax, advanced to Snickersville and Berryville and routed the enemy's cavalry (White's), capturing their colours and many prisoners.

But the cavalry took very little part in the grander movements of the army. When Sumner's grand division crossed the river on December 12th, Pleasanton's cavalry division was massed in rear of the ridge commanding the approaches to the upper bridges. And when Franklin crossed below the city, he was preceded by Bayard's cavalry division, which reconnoitered the country southward.[5] This was the extent of the cavalry operations, the exhausting and unceasing picket duty monopolizing almost the entire time and attention of officers and men.

---

5. General Bayard was killed on the 15th by a piece of shell, while near General Franklin's headquarters. He was succeeded by Colonel D. McM. Gregg, Eighth Pennsylvania Cavalry; and Colonel Thomas C. Devin succeeded to the command of the Second Brigade of Pleasanton's division. Both these officers were destined to become celebrated in the subsequent operations of the cavalry. For the organization of the cavalry at Fredericksburg, see Appendix 8.

After the Union army fell back across the Rappahannock, the two armies confronted each other, each endeavouring to recuperate from the terrible struggle at Fredericksburg, and each hesitating to take the initiative. There were dissensions in the Army of the Potomac, and differences of opinion. Burnside was for a general advance, but was opposed in this by his grand division commanders. And the commanding general's views so far took shape that a cavalry expedition, proposed and organized by General Averell, was put on foot (December 28th), only to be recalled at the last moment by orders from the President, instigated by general officers, who differed with General Burnside as to the wisdom of aggressive action at this time.

Averell proposed to take a thousand picked men, selected from nine regiments, with four pieces of artillery, proceed by Kelly's Ford on the Rappahannock and Raccoon Ford on the Rapidan to the James River, and by crossing on the bridge at Carterville, to proceed to Suffolk, or join the Federal forces in North Carolina, under General Foster. The expedition was expected to destroy the railroads, bridges, and telegraph lines between the Federal army and Richmond, and was to depend upon the country for sustenance. In many respects it did not differ in conception from the Stoneman raid of six months later.

CHAPTER 4

Kelly's Ford to Scott's Run

On January 26th, General Burnside was relieved from command of the Army of the Potomac, and was succeeded by General Hooker. A few days later (February 6, 1863) the organization by grand divisions was abolished, and that by army corps substituted, with General Stoneman to command all the cavalry.

This consolidation of the cavalry was by far the most important step that had yet been taken to increase its efficiency, and enable it to act in its true role.

The cavalry corps was organized in three divisions, commanded by Generals Pleasanton, Averell, and Gregg, with the Reserve Brigade in command of General Buford. On February 10, 1863, the corps had an aggregate of 13,452 officers and men present for duty the present and absent numbering 17,166. These figures give some idea of the large number of absentees. The regular regiments, especially, were depleted in numbers. Regular officers were constantly as signed to duty with volunteer commands, as well as to many staff positions; and in the matter of recruiting the Government could not successfully compete with the States. At times the strength of the regular regiments did not average more than 250 men present for duty. A squadron the tactical unit of organization contained anywhere from sixty to one hundred men, and was only brought up to the required strength by the addition of extra companies.

During the months of January and February the cavalry was kept constantly employed, reconnoitering the enemy's position, watching the fords of the Rappahannock, and engaged in almost constant skirmishing.[1] Much of this was done in severe winter weather, while the infantry was being made comfortable in winter quarters.

The enemy's cavalry was very bold and aggressive. On February 24th General Fitzhugh Lee, with 400 of his cavalry, crossed the river at Kelly's Ford, drove back the Federal pickets at Hartwood Church, and brought on a skirmish with Averell's cavalry. Under the impression that the enemy were in force, General Stoneman immediately put the divisions of Pleasanton and Averell in motion, followed by the Reserve Brigade; but after encamping for a night at Morrisville, the enemy eluded their pursuers by recrossing the Rappahannock.

On March 17th, however, an engagement was fought at Kelly's Ford, which made the Confederate cavalry more wary, and did much towards making the Union cavalry more aggressive.

General Averell received orders to cross the river with 3,000 cavalry and six pieces of artillery, and attack and destroy the forces of General Fitzhugh Lee, supposed to be near Culpeper Court House.

The Union general started from Morrisville with about 2,100 men all told, and arriving at Kelly's Ford, found the crossing obstructed with abatis, and defended by about eighty sharpshooters, covered by rifle-pits and houses on the opposite bank. After several attempts, the crossing was gallantly effected by Lieutenant Brown with 20 men of the First Rhode Island Cavalry, who took twenty-five prison-

---

1. At Grove Church, Fairfax, Middleburg, Rappahannock Bridge, Somerville.

ers. The crossing could easily have been forced by the use of artillery, but it was not desired to give notice of the movement to the enemy.

Westward from the ford, the ground was comparatively clear for half a mile, followed by woods; and beyond the latter was an open field. The cavalry column reached the first line of woods without opposition, when the enemy was discovered advancing in line. The Fourth New York was directed to form line to the right of the road, the Fourth Pennsylvania to the left, with a section of artillery between the two. In front of these troops was a broad, deep ditch, covered by a heavy stone wall; and from behind this obstacle the carbines of the cavalry and guns of the artillery delivered a brisk fire. Farther to the right the Third Pennsylvania and Sixteenth Pennsylvania had come into position; while to the left the First Rhode Island and Sixth Ohio had also formed line. As the enemy advanced under the galling fire of the dismounted men, Colonel Duffié, commanding the first brigade, led the regiments on the left of the line in a most successful charge. This charge was closely followed by that of Colonel McIntosh, who struck the left flank of another of the enemy's columns just arriving on the field, and the entire body of Confederate cavalry was driven back in great confusion.

The Federal line being re-formed, it again advanced three-quarters of a mile, driving the enemy through a second line of woods. Beyond these woods, and distant about half a mile, the Confederates made another stand, and attempted to advance under cover of a heavy artillery fire, but were again repulsed and driven from the field. As it was then quite late in the day, and the horses of the Federal cavalry were much exhausted, the division was withdrawn, and recrossed Kelly's Ford without opposition. The official return of casualties was, for the Union forces, 78; and for the Confederates, 133,

This engagement has been described with some degree of detail, because of its importance as being the first time the Federal cavalry was made to feel its superiority, or at least equality, with the splendid cavalry of Stuart.[2] It was another step in the increasing feeling of confidence in themselves and in their leaders, which was to manifest itself in a still greater degree at the subsequent battle of Brandy Station.

But the interminable picket duty of the cavalry still went on,[3] as though none but mounted troops were capable of performing such service.

During this period, too, the Federal cavalry in West Virginia were kept more than usually busy, due to the expedition of the Confederate General Imboden into that State (April 20th to May 14th), and also the raid of General W. E. Jones on the Baltimore & Ohio Railroad (April 21st to May 21st), leading to skirmishes at Beverly, Janelew, and Summerville, W. Va.

In addition to these attempts to frustrate the more important raids of Confederate troops in the State, the Union cavalry in West Virginia had particularly arduous service during the entire year, in attempts to break up the depredations of the guerrilla bands of Mosby and Gilmore. During the winter of 1862-63 movements of troops were especially onerous on account of the severity of the winter weather in the mountains, and the extent of the territory to be guarded.

During the spring of 1863, as well as during the suc-

---

2. Generals Stuart's and Fitzhugh Lee's official reports of this engagement dwell on the fact that the Union forces were afraid to meet their opponents in the open, and that the mounted troops continually fell back, when hard pressed, to the protection of their artillery and dismounted skirmishers.

3. The skirmishes of the cavalry while upon this duty were of daily occurrence, some of them very severe — Bealeton Station, Herndon, Occoquon, Little River Turnpike, Broad Run. Middleburg, Burlington. Purgitsville, Rappahannock Bridge. Kelly's, Welford's, and Beverly fords. (Skirmish of April 14-15.)

ceeding summer, the cavalry in West Virginia fought a number of minor skirmishes, which, though often bravely contested, reflected no great credit on the cavalry arm. As General Halleck states in his report (November 15, 1863): "The force [in West Virginia], being too small to attempt any campaign by itself, has acted merely on the defensive in repelling raids and breaking up guerrilla bands."

The same may be said of the cavalry of General Milroy, operating in the Shenandoah Valley at this time. Though kept continually busy, reconnoitering, patrolling, and picketing this part of Virginia, its operations were of a minor character.[4]

On April 27, 1863, was inaugurated the Chancellorsville campaign, General Hooker crossing the Rappahannock and Rapidan above their junction. At the same time the major portion of the cavalry corps under Stoneman crossed the upper Rappahannock for a raid on the enemy's communications with Richmond.

Stoneman's instructions from Hooker were framed with the idea in view that the coming encounter between the Army of the Potomac and the Army of Northern Virginia would be gained by the Federal army.

"You will march," says the order, "with all your available force, except one brigade, for the purpose of turning the enemy's position on his left, and of throwing your command between him and Richmond, and isolating him from his supplies, checking his retreat, and inflicting on him every possible injury which will tend to his discomfiture and defeat. You may rely upon the General [Hooker] being in connection with you before your supplies are exhausted.

Leaving Devin's brigade of Pleasanton s division for duty with the Army of the Potomac, Stoneman crossed the Rappahannock on April 29th, by way of the railroad bridge and Kelly's Ford. Three days rations and three days allowance of

---

4. The cavalry fought skirmishes at Buck's, Front Royal, and Berry's fords.

short forage were taken on the troopers horses; while three days subsistence and two days short forage were taken upon pack-mules. With the exception of the artillery, not a wheel of any description accompanied the command.

After crossing the river, General Stoneman turned over to Averell's command which consisted of one division, one brigade, and six pieces of artillery the task of defeating any force of the enemy likely to impede the operations of the raiding force. But Averell had not gone far when he was re-called by an order from General Hooker, leaving Stoneman with one division, one brigade, and six pieces of artillery, aggregating 4,329 men.

The Rapidan was crossed at Morton's and Raccoon Fords on the 30th, and thereafter, until May 8th, the command subsisted entirely on the country through which it passed. After taking possession of Louisa Court House, Stoneman passed on and destroyed the Virginia Central Railroad from Gordonsville, for eighteen miles eastward, together with all railroad bridges, trains, depôts, provisions, and telegraph lines. Passing on, a large portion of the Aquia & Richmond Railroad was destroyed, all the bridges across the South Anna, and several across the North Anna.

On May 3rd Colonel Judson Kilpatrick, commanding one of the brigades, was sent with his own regiment (Harris Light) to destroy the railroad bridge over the Chicka-hominy. But, being unable to rejoin Stoneman, Kilpatrick took refuge within the Union lines on the Peninsula, hav-ing burned the bridge over the Chickahominy, run a train of cars into the river, destroyed the ferry at Hanovertown in time to check a pursuing force, surprised a Confeder-ate force at Aylett's, burned fifty-six wagons and a depôt containing 60,000 bushels of corn, and destroyed the ferry over the Mattapony, as well as vast quantities of clothing and commissary stores.

As to Stoneman's main command, the six days having expired during which General Hooker was to have opened communication, and supplies becoming scarce, Stoneman decided to make the best of his way to the Army of the Potomac, which he reached in safety. He then learned the result of the sanguinary battle of Chancellorsville.[5]

As a moral factor and an engine of destruction, the Stoneman raid was a great success. It destroyed millions of dollars worth of Confederate property, and, although for a short time only, cut Lee's communications. Its moral effect, judging from the Confederate correspondence since published, was much greater than was at the time believed to be the case. It, more over, taught the Union cavalry how to cut loose from their base of supplies, and gave them a new confidence in their mobility never before experienced.

But, as a part of the main operations, the raid was ill-timed. Its complete success, depending as it did on a Federal victory at Chancellorsville, was frustrated through no fault of the cavalry or its commander. The detaching of Stoneman's command deprived Hooker of cavalry at a time when he particularly needed a covering force to conceal the movements of his right, as well as to give timely information of the Confederate concentration against his right flank. The Comte de Paris has said: "The absence of Stoneman's fine cavalry had probably been the cause of Hooker's defeat, as he had deprived himself of all means of obtaining information when about to enter an impenetrable forest. Such was Jackson's opinion, expressed a few days before his death. From the moment he [Hooker] had failed to compel Lee to retreat, the role assigned to Stoneman lost almost all its importance.[6]

But the cavalry brigade left with the Army of the Potomac performed most valuable service.

---

5. For organization of cavalry, see Appendix 9.
6. *History of the Civil War*, Vol. 4., page 115. (Comte de Paris.)

On May 2nd General Lee, having concluded that a direct attack upon the Union forces would prove futile, determined to turn the Federal right flank, and its execution was entrusted to General T. J. Jackson. By a flank march along the Furnace and Brock road, effectually covered by the heavy woods and by the movements of Fitzhugh Lee's cavalry, Jackson succeeded in placing three divisions opposite the Union right.

On the afternoon of this day General Pleasanton, with three small cavalry regiments, the Sixth New York, Eighth Pennsylvania, and Seventeenth Pennsylvania, was ordered to assist General Sickles in pursuing the enemy's wagon trains. Finding the time inopportune for a cavalry attack, Pleasanton took position north of Scott's Run, on the left of the Eleventh Corps (Howard's).

Jackson's attack on this corps was a complete surprise, and resulted in a demoralizing and panic-stricken retreat on its part. As this was taking place, Pleasanton was notified, and the Eighth Pennsylvania Cavalry was dispatched at a gallop to check the enemy's attack at any cost, until preparations could be made to receive them. When this regiment reached the scene of action,[7] Howard had fallen back, and the enemy s skirmish line had crossed the road along which the cavalry was moving. Led by Colonel Huey, the regiment made a desperate charge in column, at right angles to Jackson's column, losing three officers out of the five with the regiment, and about thirty men, but checking for the time being the Confederate advance.

Meanwhile Pleasanton, to whom every moment's delay was invaluable, had been straining every effort to concentrate artillery to meet the advancing lines, and before the enemy came in sight, had succeeded in placing twenty-three pieces of artillery in position, double-shotted with

7. *Huey's report, Rebellion Records,* Vol. 25., Part 1., page 784.

canister, and supported by two small cavalry squadrons. The fugitives from the Eleventh Corps swarmed from the woods, and swept frantically over the fields, the exulting enemy at their heels. But as the latter drew near, the Federal artillery opened with terrible effect. The Confederate lines were thrown back in disorder and with the arrival of reinforcements to the Union line, aided by darkness, the enemy withdrew.

It is impossible to say what might have happened had not the attack of Jackson's victorious divisions been checked. The sacrifice of the brave cavalry regiment well repaid the results gained, and illustrates how very effective as a gainer of time the charge in flank of even a small body of cavalry may be, when prosecuted with vigour. It was, perhaps, the most important piece of mounted work by a single cavalry regiment during the entire war.

CHAPTER 6

Chancellorsville to Brandy Station

After Chancellorsville the opposing armies rested for a time on opposite sides of the Rappahannock, near Fredericksburg.

During the entire month of May the cavalry was greatly annoyed by Mosby's men. On the 3rd Mosby and others surrounded fifty men of the First West Virginia, but the latter were rescued by a brilliant charge of the Fifth New York. Towards the middle of the month the First New York had a skirmish with a portion of Mosby's command at Upperville (May 12-14); and again on the 30th Mosby attacked the train of the Eighth Michigan near Catlett's Station, burning it and engaging in a spirited cavalry fight with the First Vermont, Fifth New York, and a detachment of the Seventh Michigan. Partly as an offset to these raids, the Eighth Illinois Cavalry was sent on a raiding expedition (May 20-26) into King George, Westmoreland, Richmond, Northumberland, and Lancaster counties, destroying property estimated at one million dollars.

Early in June Stuart's cavalry were holding the fords of the upper Rappahannock, the main body being near Culpeper Court House and Brandy Station. It retained its division organization, being composed of five brigades, aggregating May 31st, 9,536 men.

To the right rear of the Army of the Potomac was the Federal cavalry, massed at Warrenton Junction under General Pleasanton, who had May 22nd assumed command. It was still organized as a corps of three divisions, numbering in all 7,981 men, and was charged with outpost duty from the neighbourhood of Falmouth to Warrenton, with occasional expeditions into the country above the upper Rapidan.

In Lee's plan of invasion of the Northern States, his first objective was Culpeper Court House. Hooker guessed Lee's intentions, and Pleasanton was ordered to make a reconnaissance in force, having for its object to discover the strength, position, and possible intentions of any body of Confederate troops on the Fredericksburg-Culpeper road. But the corps was hampered by the addition of two infantry brigades according to the still prevailing idea as to the employment of cavalry.

On June 9th one division of the cavalry corps (Buford's), accompanied by Ames' infantry brigade, was to cross the Rappahannock at Beverly Ford, and moved by way of St. James Church to Brandy Station. The second column, Gregg's and Duffié's divisions, with Russell's infantry brigade, was to cross at Kelly's Ford, and, separating, Gregg was to proceed past Mount Dumpling to Brandy Station, while Duffié was to take the left-hand road to Stevensburg.

By a strange coincidence, it was Stuart's intention on this same day to cross the river at Beverly Ford and the upper fords, and divert the attention of the Union forces from Lee's movements northward later information showing that he intended to invade Maryland.

The orders for the Federal cavalry divisions directed them to cross the river at daylight on the 9th, and push rapidly on to Brandy Station. Under cover of a heavy fog and the noise of a neighbouring mill-dam, Buford's command crossed the river at 4 o'clock, surprised the enemy,[1] and would have captured his guns had it not been for the untimely death of the brave Colonel B. F. Davis, Eighth New York Cavalry, who was killed while charging the enemy at the head of his brigade. The enemy's force confronting the Federal column was superior in numbers, but in spite of this fact, Pleasanton had formed line of battle crossing the ford in less than an hour. But the Confederates were in such force that no advance was made until Gregg's guns were heard on the enemy's left, when a general advance was ordered.

The enemy fell back rapidly, and General Stuart's headquarters, with all his papers, was captured. A junction was soon formed with Gregg, and with heavy losses to both sides the enemy was pushed back to Fleetwood Ridge. It was then found that the enemy's infantry was advancing from Brandy Station and Culpeper. The object of the reconnaissance having been partly gained, through the development of the Confederate infantry from the direction of Culpeper, and the information gained from the papers captured in the Confederate camp, orders were given to withdraw Gregg by the way of the ford at Rappahannock Bridge, and Buford at Beverly Ford. But as this order was being put into execution, the Confederates made a heavy attack on the Union right, resulting in the most serious fighting of the day. The mounted charges, rallies, and counter charges by the cavalry of both sides made this pre-eminently a cavalry fight of the most desperate character.

At 4 o'clock p. m., a superior infantry force being about to advance, Pleasanton ordered a withdrawal, which was executed in good order, the recrossing of the river being effected about 7 o'clock p. m.

The contest had lasted for ten hours, and the casualties,

---

1. This attack was afterwards known to the Confederates as "The Surprise."

amounting to 866 for the Federal troops and 485 for the Confederates,[2] attest the desperate character of the fighting. Although the battle illustrated all kinds of cavalry fighting, mounted and dismounted, it was principally mounted. Stuart had the advantage in position, but the conditions were most favourable for cavalry operations; men and horses were in prime condition for active service; the ground was undulating, rising slightly from the river towards Brandy Station; and the infantry on both sides served principally as a reserve.

Brandy Station rounded up the successful experiences of the Federal cavalry at Kelly's Ford in March, and with the raiding column of Stoneman in April. It was the first great cavalry combat of the war, and was really the turning-point in the fortunes of the Union cavalry. The Confederate cavalry had hitherto held their opponents in contempt, and the latter had had doubts of themselves.

But the experience of June 9, 1868, made the Union cavalry, and henceforth no one could doubt its efficiency, mounted or dismounted. McClellan has said: "One result of incalculable importance certainly did follow this battle it made the Federal cavalry. Up to this time confessedly inferior to the Southern horse men, they gained on this day that confidence in them selves and their commanders which enabled them to contest so fiercely the subsequent battle-fields of June, July, and October."[3]

---

2. *Official returns, Rebellion Records,* Vol. 27, Parts 1. and 2., pages 170 and 719, respectively.
3. McClellan's *Campaign of Stuart's Cavalry*, page 294.

CHAPTER 7

Aldie to Upperville

Lee's second objective was the fords of the upper Potomac, and these he proposed to reach by the valley of the Shenandoah, where, concealed from observation by the mountain ranges on his right, his safety, could be secured by holding the mountain passes connecting the valley with the main theatre of operations. He entrusted this duty to Stuart's cavalry, supported by Longstreet's infantry corps.

By June 15th Stuart had pushed forward to the Bull Run Mountains, and held Thoroughfare and Aldie gaps, traversed respectively by the main road from Winchester to Alexandria, and the Manassas Gap Railway. He also occupied Rectortown, and, later on, Middleburg, from which points he could reinforce either one of the two passes, as occasion required.

On June 13th the cavalry corps of the Army of the Potomac was concentrated at Warrenton Junction, and from the 14th to the 17th, was covering the movement of the main army northward.

Lee's movements were, however, so well concealed that on the 17th the cavalry corps was sent to obtain information. This was one of the very things that Stuart had been instructed to prevent.

Pleasanton proposed to move to Ashby's Gap in the Blue

Ridge, by way of Aldie. To do this, he moved on Aldie with Buford's and Gregg's divisions Barnes division of infantry in support and detached Duffié with his regiment, the First Rhode Island Cavalry, to march to Middleburg, by way of Thoroughfare Gap. It was expected that Duffié would rejoin the main command, after it had passed through Aldie, by way of Union, Purcellville, and Nolan's Ferry.

Munford's brigade of Stuart's cavalry was at Aldie, and Gregg's division encountered his outposts on the 17th inst. A spirited engagement ensued, in which the advantage remained with the Federal cavalry, the enemy withdrawing from the field and occupying Middleburg that night. The casualties were quite heavy on both sides, aggregating for the Federal troops 305 killed, wounded, and missing, and for the Confederates 119. There was much mounted and dismounted fighting on both sides, the greater number of casualties on the Federal side being due to the obstinate resistance of the Confederate sharpshooters, posted behind stonewalls. Stuart, in his report of the engagement, pronounced Aldie "one of the most sanguinary battles of the war."

Meanwhile Duffié had proceeded through Thorough fare Gap, where he encountered the enemy's outposts. As his orders directed him to proceed to Middleburg, he kept on, and was ultimately surrounded by Chambliss' and Robertson's Confederate brigades. Duffié, with four officers and twenty-seven men only, succeeded in escaping.

On the 19th Pleasanton advanced against the Confederates at Middleburg. Three brigades under Gregg moved on the town, while one brigade was sent to out flank the enemy's position. The fighting was of the most desperate character, the Federal forces, as Pleasanton stated in a letter to Hooker, "really fighting infantry behind stone walls." The enemy's right flank was finally outflanked by dismounted skirmishers and fell back to a stronger position, half a mile to the rear.

The same evening Stuart was reinforced by Jones' brigade from Union; and on the 20th, by Hampton's brigade, which relieved Chambliss on the Upperville road.

On the 21st Stuart's line of five brigades extended from Middleburg to Union, confronted by six brigades of Federal cavalry, supported by a division of infantry. Gregg's division moved against the enemy's right, while Buford's advanced toward Union to turn the Confederate left. As so often happened, Gregg's movement, though intended as a feint only, developed into the principal fight of the day. Protected by the heights, the enemy stubbornly resisted Gregg's advance, but were steadily driven back to Upperville, where the first division (Buford's), which had closed in on the second division on its left, cooperated with it in the attack on the town. Here the enemy had massed his cavalry, with his artillery in position at Ashby's Gap; but after repeated charges and counter-charges, was driven from the town, and his steady withdrawal was finally changed to a headlong retreat towards Ashby's Gap.[1]

That night a portion of Longstreet's infantry corps occupied the gap; and Stuart's command, as that general says in his report, was "ordered farther back for rest and refreshment, of which it was sorely in need." And on June 22nd, having accomplished the objects of the expedition, Pleasanton fell back to Aldie, and a few days later joined the Army of the Potomac.

In these operations the cavalry corps had admirably performed the duties of screening the movements of the Army of the Potomac and of reconnoitering the enemy's movements. Some of Buford's scouts on the heights of the Blue Ridge had actually seen a Confederate infantry camp, two miles in length, in the valley of the Shenandoah. At

---

1. Casualties at Upperville: Union, 209. Upperville and. Middleburg (consolidated): Confederate, 510.

the same time, Lee was uncertain of the movements of the Army of the Potomac. The success of the engagements at Aldie, Middleburg, and Upperville brought increasing confidence to the officers and men of the Federal cavalry.

Within five days it had driven the Confederate cavalry through a country capable of a most stubborn defence, as far as the base of the Blue Ridge; had proved its ability to cope, mounted or dismounted, with its formidable antagonists; and had been able to furnish information of a most important character to the commander-in-chief.

During this time the Army of the Potomac had, under cover of the cavalry, moved from Fredericksburg northward, covering Washington and Baltimore, and on June 25th and 26th had crossed the Potomac at Edwards Ferry. Upon reaching Frederick, General Hooker was, at his own request, relieved from command of the army, and General Meade was appointed in his stead.

When Pleasanton, on June 22nd, withdrew from contact with the enemy he employed the few days in which his corps was on outpost duty in refitting. His horses needed shoeing badly, and his command required both rations and forage. On June 27th the divisions of Buford and Gregg crossed the Potomac in rear of the infantry, and on the following day a new cavalry division, composed of the cavalry hitherto guarding Washington under General Stahel, was assigned to the cavalry corps as the Third Division. General Judson Kilpatrick was assigned to command it, with Generals Farnsworth (an officer promoted from the Eighth Illinois Volunteer Cavalry) and Custer as his brigade commanders.[2]

---

2. For the organization of the cavalry at Gettysburg, July 1st to 3rd, see Appendix 10 and 11.

CHAPTER 8

Stuart & Buford

On June 24th Stuart's cavalry started on a raid which was destined to have a most important effect upon the battle of Gettysburg, about to follow. Its purpose was to cut the communications of the Federal army, destroy the immense wagon trains in rear of that army, and create a moral effect by threatening the national capital.

General Lee's letter to Stuart, dated June 22nd, gives him these general instructions: "If you find that he [the enemy] is moving northward, and that two brigades can guard the Blue Ridge and take care of your rear, you can move with the other three into Maryland, and take position on General Ewell's right."

And again, in a letter written to Stuart the following day, Lee says: "You will, however, be able to judge whether you can pass around their army without hindrance, doing them all the damage you can, and cross the river east of the mountains. In either case, after crossing the river, you must move on and feel the right of Ewell's troops."

It seems, from these letters and confirmatory statements in letters to General Longstreet, that Lee authorized, if he did not actually suggest, Stuart's raid about the Federal army. But, while giving Stuart great discretionary power, he qualified this power by several important conditions. That

Stuart met with hindrances which prevented his keeping in touch with Ewell's right, and even caused his absence from part of the battle of Gettysburg, is a matter of history.

Taking the brigades of Fitzhugh Lee, Hampton, and Chambliss, Stuart moved on June 25th to Haymarket, *via* Glassoock's Gap, where he was delayed twenty-four hours by encountering Hancock's corps of infantry. On the 27th he crossed the Potomac at Bowser's Ford, and on the following day captured a Federal wagon train eight miles long.

On this same day the cavalry corps of the Army of the Potomac was disposed so that Gregg was on the right, Buford on the left, and Kilpatrick in advance. In consequence of Stuart's depredations, Kilpatrick's division was on June 28th detached, and ordered to move eastward to intercept Stuart, reported to be heading for Littlestown. By June 30th Kilpatrick's command was badly scattered, the First and Second Michigan and Pennington's battery being at Abbottstown, north of Hanover, and Farnsworth's brigade was at Littlestown, south-west of Hanover. The Fifth and Sixth Michigan readied Littlestown at daylight, after an all-night march, and during the morning Farnsworth started towards Hanover. The troops at Abbottstown were also ordered there.

As Farnsworth passed through Hanover, his rear guard was attacked by the leading regiment of Stuart's column (Chambliss' brigade), which boldly charged and threw the Federal column into great confusion, capturing the pack-trains. Under Farnsworth's skillful direction, however, the Fifth New York Cavalry was faced about, and by a counter-charge repulsed the attack. Meanwhile the Sixth Michigan, which had been left for awhile at Littlestown, was hurried up, and was attacked *en route* by Fitzhugh Lee's brigade. About noon the entire division was united at Hanover, and until dark kept up a vigorous skirmishing with the enemy, now holding the hills south-west of the town.

Stuart's dispositions, in guarding the long line of wagons he had captured, were such as to prevent his rapid deployment. Otherwise he might have overcome the rear of Kilpatrick's column before it could have been reinforced. As it was, Stuart's elongated column gave a fine opportunity for a successful attack by the Federal commander, which he failed to take complete advantage of, principally because he was unable to concentrate his scattered units. But Kilpatrick's final stand had the effect of still further delaying Stuart's efforts to join Lee.

This encounter, coupled with his efforts to save the wagon train which embarrassed his movements, and the fact that he believed Lee to be near the Susquehanna, forced Stuart to make a detour to the east, passing through Jefferson and Dover, and endeavouring to carry out his original instructions as to keeping in touch with Ewell's right. Swinging northward to Carlisle on July 1st, Stuart learned, to his dismay, that the Confederate army was at Gettysburg, and that, in spite of the exhausted condition of his command, he must push south ward with all haste, in order to be present at the expected encounter of the two great armies. He therefore moved rapidly towards Gettysburg, while Kilpatrick, who had meanwhile been acting on interior lines, marched to Berlin, by way of Abbottstown, for the purpose of throwing himself across Stuart's path, but the Confederate commander succeeded in eluding him.

While Kilpatrick had been following Stuart, the First Cavalry Division (Buford's) had marched to Middletown, covering the left of the army, and watching the enemy in the direction of Hagerstown. While in camp at Middletown, Buford improved the opportunity to shoe his horses and refit. The second division (Gregg's) was stationed at different points from Frederick City to Ridgeville on the Baltimore pike, covering the right of the army.

On June 29th the first division moved so as to cover and protect the left flank of the line of march, the Reserve Brigade, under Merritt, marching through Mechanicstown to Emmittsburg, protecting the division trains, while the First and Second Brigades, passing through Boonesborough, Cavetown, and Monterey, encamped at Fairfield. The Second Cavalry Division on that day moved to Westminster on the right flank of the army, patrolling the country between York and Carlisle.

On June 30th Buford's first and second brigades moved towards Gettysburg, meeting *en route* two Confederate infantry regiments, with artillery, and became involved in a skirmish. But not wishing to use his artillery, lest he cause a premature concentration of the enemy's forces, and thus disarrange General Meade's plans, Buford turned aside, and, passing through Emmittsburg, reached Gettysburg during the afternoon. His arrival was most timely. The enemy's advance was just entering the town, and Buford was able to drive it back in the direction of Cashtown before it gained a foothold.

During the night of June 30th scouting parties from Buford's division patrolled the country in all directions.

No information of value could be obtained from the inhabitants, and it was only through the untiring exertions of these patrols that the cavalry commander learned by daylight of July 1st that Hill's corps of the Confederate army had reached Cashtown, and that his pickets, composed of infantry and artillery, were within sight of the Federal pickets. Buford accordingly made every effort to hold the enemy in check until Reynolds corps, encamped five miles south of him, could arrive on the ground. His trained eye had been struck at once with the strategic importance of Gettysburg. From the town at least ten roads radiated in different directions, and the commanding ground above the town offered extraordinary advantages to the army which should first gain possession. It seems apparent that neither General Lee nor General Meade were at the time aware of the strategic importance of the place.[1] To Buford belongs the credit of the selection of Gettysburg as a field of battle,[2] and the cool equanimity with which he disposed his two insignificant brigades, when he positively knew that the whole of General A. P. Hill's force was advancing against him, must excite the admiration of soldiers the world over.

---

1. Meade's dispatch to Reynolds, 11:30 a. m., June 30th: "P. S. If, after occupying your present position, it is your judgement that you would be in better position at Emmittsburg than where you are, you can fall back without waiting for the enemy or further orders. Your present position was given more with a view to an advance on Gettysburg than a defensive point." Then again, Reynolds dispatch to Butterfield, June 30th: "I think if the enemy advances in force from Gettysburg, and we are to fight a defensive battle in this vicinity, that the position to be occupied is just north of the town of Emmittsburg. covering the plank road to Taneytown."
2. Buford stated to his brigade commander, Devin, "that the battle would be fought at that point" (Gettysburg). And again, "The enemy must know the importance of this position, and will strain every nerve to secure it, and if we are able to hold it, we would do well." (Bates' *Battle of Gettysburg*.)

CHAPTER 9

Gettysburg

Buford had placed Gamble's brigade, to which was attached Calef's battery of the Second U. S. Artillery, on the
left, connecting with Devin's brigade across the Chambersburg road, about one mile in front of the seminary. One
section of Calef's battery was placed on each side of the
Cashtown road, covering the approaches, and the third section was on the right of the left regiment. Devin's brigade
was on the left of the First Brigade, its right resting on the
Mummasburg road.

Between 8 and 9 o'clock in the morning Heth's division of the Confederate army advanced along the Cashtown road, and Buford sent a squadron from each brigade,
part of which was dismounted, to deploy as skirmishers
and support the pickets. Gradually the whole of the cavalry,
dismounted, became involved, and as Buford has said: "The
line of battle moved off proudly to meet the enemy." In a
short time, the enemy's fire becoming unbearable through
ever-increasing numbers, the line of battle was moved back
about 200 yards. Here again the dismounted cavalry fought
desperately, and Calef's battery did tremendous execution
in the face of an overwhelming fire. Indeed, at one time
twelve of the enemy's guns were concentrated on this battery. For over two hours the enemy was held in check by

this little force of less than 3,000 effective men, when the arrival of the First Corps, under General Reynolds, served to relieve the cavalry from its perilous position. During the greater part of the remainder of the day, however, the cavalry continued to fight side by side with the infantry; and portions of the Eighth New York, Third Indiana, and Twelfth Illinois regiments, posted behind a low stone wall within short carbine range of the enemy, did tremendous execution and by their fire prevented the turning of the left flank of General Doubleday's command.[1] Part of the Third Indiana Cavalry found horse-holders, borrowed muskets, and fought with the Wisconsin regiment that was sent to relieve them.

The First Cavalry Division bivouacked that night on the field of battle, with its pickets extending almost to Fairfield. Early next morning, while reconnoitering the enemy's right, it became engaged with Confederate sharpshooters, but succeeded in holding its position until relieved by the Third Corps. Then, at the risk of leaving the Federal army's left flank unprotected by cavalry, it was ordered to proceed to Westminster to assist in guarding the supply trains at that point.

Meanwhile the Second Cavalry Division under Gregg had been moving along the right flank of the Federal army. On June 29th it covered the country between York and Carlisle with patrols. On the 30th, due to the enemy's concentration at Gettysburg, it left one brigade (Huey's) to cover the depôt at Westminster, and with the two other brigades moved to a position on the extreme right flank of the Federal line of battle, with orders to prevent the enemy from turning the flank or gaining the rear.

---

1. General Gamble's report says: "The stand which we made against the enemy prevented our left from being turned, and saved a division of our infantry."

The position of this division at the intersection of the Gettysburg and Hanover turnpike with the road in rear of the Federal line of battle was taken about noon July 2nd. A line of pickets was established to the front, connecting with the right of the infantry line. Towards evening an attempt was made to dislodge some of the enemy's sharpshooters posted in front of the division, resulting in the enemy s sending a regiment of infantry (Second Virginia) to meet the dismounted cavalry. The key to the position was a well-built stone wall running along the top of the ridge, to the right of the Hanover road. Each side raced for the wall at full speed, but the fire from Bank's battery, Third Pennsylvania Artillery, delayed the enemy long enough for the dismounted cavalry to reach the wall first and pour a withering fire from their breech-loading carbines into the Confederate infantry line, not more than twenty feet distant. The result was decisive.

The following day, July 3rd, this cavalry division, which had for a time been withdrawn from its position of the previous day, was again ordered to the right of the line, with orders to make a demonstration against the enemy. The First and Third Brigades were again posted on the right of the infantry, this time about three-fourths of a mile nearer the Baltimore and Gettysburg turnpike, for the reason that Custer's brigade of the Third Cavalry Division had been detached from that division and was occupying the ground held the day before by the Second Cavalry Division. Dismounted skirmishers from the Sixteenth Pennsylvania Cavalry were deployed through the woods in the direction of Gettysburg.

About noon a dispatch reached General Gregg, saying that a large body of the enemy's cavalry were observed from Cemetery Hill, and were moving against the right of the line. In consequence of this information, Custer's brigade, which had been ordered back to Kilpatrick's command on the left of the line, was held by General Gregg until after the enemy's attack.

This Confederate column, moving to the attack, was Stuart's cavalry, which, belated by obstacles already mentioned, was advancing in front of Ewell's corps. Stuart took position upon a ridge which controlled a wide area of cultivated fields. His plan; as stated in his official report, was to employ the Federal troops in front with sharpshooters, while a cavalry force was moved against their flank. He says: "I moved this command [Jenkins' cavalry brigade] and W. H. F. Lee's secretly through the woods to a position, and hoped to effect a surprise upon the enemy's rear." Taken in combination with Pickett's famous charge, Stuart's dispositions were such that he hoped to seize the opportune moment to profit by it.

To meet this attack the First New Jersey was posted as mounted skirmishers to the right and front in a wood; the Third Pennsylvania was deployed as dismounted skirmishers to the left and front in open fields and the First Maryland Cavalry was placed on the Hanover turnpike, in position to protect the right of the line.

In a short time the skirmishing became very brisk, and the artillery fire on both sides very heavy the Federal artillery under Randall and Pennington, delivering an extremely accurate fire. To counteract the advance of the Federal skirmish line, about to cut off a portion of his sharpshooters, Stuart caused a regiment of W. H. F. Lee's brigade to charge. This was met by the Seventh Michigan, but without apparent advantage, both regiments discharging their carbines across a stone-and-rail fence, face to face. The First Michigan Cavalry, aided by firing from Chester's battery, made a charge which, followed by a desperate hand-to-hand fight, drove the Confederate line back in confusion. Then followed counter-charges by the Confederates, until a large part of both commands were involved in the *mêlée*, and while withdrawing past a wood towards his left the enemy was charged in flank by the First New Jersey Cavalry. In this terrible cavalry combat, every possible weapon was utilized. In a dash for a Confederate battle-flag Captain Newhall was received by its bearer upon the point of the spear-head, which hurled Newhall to the ground. And after the battle men were found interlocked in each other's arms, with fingers so firmly embedded in the flesh as to require force to remove them.[2] The Confederate brigades crumbled away, retiring behind their artillery, and after dark withdrew to the York road. The Federal casualties had amounted to 254, and the Confederate to 181.[3]

This grand cavalry combat,[4] on the right of the Federal line of battle, has, like Buford's glorious stand in the first day's fight, never received the recognition which its importance deserved. Had Stuart's plan of striking the rear of the Union army simultaneously with the desperate charge of Pickett on Cemetery Ridge succeeded, the result of the battle of Gettysburg would certainly have been different.

The occasion for Stuart's attack was most opportune. The tide of battle between the long lines of infantry had been wavering, first one way and then the other. Had Stuart, with his veteran cavalry, gained the rear of the line of battle, the panic which would have undoubtedly followed would have been more than sufficient to win the day for the Confederate cause.

---

2. *Battles and Leaders of the Civil War,* Vol. 3., p. 405.
3. *Rebellion Records,* Vol. 27., Part 1., p. 958; Part 2., p. 714. *Gregg's Fight at Gettysburg.* (*Battles and Leaders of the Civil War.*)
4. Known as Rummel's Farm.

CHAPTER 10

Day Two—Farnsworth's Charge

On the Federal left another great cavalry battle was taking place. After Kilpatrick's encounter with Stuart's cavalry at Hanover, June 30th. it will be remembered that the Third Cavalry Division marched on the following day to Berlin via Abbottstown, for the purpose of intercepting Stuart. Not finding him there, a detachment under Lieutenant-Colonel Alexander followed Stuart to Rossville. On July 2nd, the second day of the battle of Gettysburg, Kilpatrick received orders to march as quickly as possible to the battle-field. Here he received further orders to move over the Gettysburg- Abbottstown road, and see that the enemy did not turn the Federal left flank. While nearing Hunterstown, Kilpatrick was attacked by a heavy cavalry force in position, which proved to be Hampton's and Lee's brigades. Custer, whose brigade was leading, at once covered the road with a line of mounted skirmishers, while dismounted skirmishers were thrown out on each side behind the fences which flanked the road. The leading squadron of the Sixth Michigan Cavalry charged down the road, and two squadrons were dismounted and deployed along a ridge to the right. Pennington's battery took position to their rear. This gallant charge of the leading squadron was futile against the superior force which it encountered, but it gained time. A counter-charge, which the enemy attempted, was repelled by the dismounted skirmishers with their Spencer repeating carbines.

The position was held until near midnight, when Kilpatrick received orders to march to Two Taverns. Reaching there early in the morning of July 3rd, the tired troopers were allowed a short bivouac. But hardly had the men of Custer's brigade stretched themselves on the ground, when orders arrived, detaching them. and directing the brigade to take position on the Union right,[1] where, as has been seen, they rendered such signal aid to the Second Cavalry Division.

The Union left had been deprived of protection by the detaching of Buford's division to Westminster on July 2nd; so that at 8 o'clock the morning of July 3rd Kilpatrick received orders from General Pleasanton to move to the left of the line with his whole command and the Reserve Brigade, meanwhile ordered up from Emmittsburg. The purpose was to attack the enemy's right and rear, at the same time preventing, if possible, the turning of the Federal left.

The result of the Confederate operations of the day before had induced them to believe that another attack on the Federal right would succeed. The column of attack was to consist of Pickett's, Heth's, and a part of Fender's divisions, Pickett being on the right.

General Farnsworth reached his position to the left and front of the "Round Tops" about 1 o'clock p. m. and became engaged with his skirmishers, the Confederate division immediately opposed to him being Hood's division

---

1. Kilpatrick's report characterizes this detaching of Custer's brigade as "a mistake." Gregg's report: "I learned that the Second Brigade of the Third Division was occupying my position of the day before," which seems to indicate that Gregg was not responsible for the detaching of Custer. Pleasanton's report, too, gives no clue as to who detached this brigade. At all events, the detaching of Custer, whether due to mistake or to wise forethought, was of the greatest assistance in preventing Stuart's attempted turning movement.

under General Law. About this time (1 o'clock) began the grand cannonade from one hundred and twenty-five pieces of artillery, which was to precede the assault of the Confederate infantry column. The arrival of Farnsworth's brigade had the effect of constantly threatening Law's right, and greatly embarrassed that general's movements.[2]

Meanwhile, the Reserve Brigade under Merritt, having marched from Emmittsburg, did not reach its position on Farnsworth's left until about 3 o'clock. Then, advancing along the Gettysburg road, Merritt s dismounted skirmishers caused Law to detach a large force from his main line in order to protect his flank and rear. This so weakened the Confederate line in Farnsworth's front that Kilpatrick ordered Farnsworth to charge the centre of Law's line. The ground was most unfavourable for a charge, being broken, uneven, and covered with stone. It was, moreover, intersected by fences and stone walls, some of the latter being so high as to preclude the possibility of passing them without dismounting and throwing them down. Posted behind these fences and walls were veteran infantry.

After making a dignified protest against what he considered a most reckless sacrifice of life, Farnsworth placed himself at the head of his brigade, and rode, as became a brave soldier and gallant cavalryman, boldly to his death.[3] When his body was afterwards recovered, it was found to have received five mortal wounds.

---

2. General Law regarded the appearance of the cavalry as exceedingly dangerous to his flank. He says (*Battles and Leaders of the Civil War*, Century Company): "While the artillery duel was in progress, and before our infantry had moved to the attack, a new danger threatened us on the right. This was the appearance of Kilpatrick's division of cavalry, which moved up on that flank, and commenced massing in the body of the timber which extended from the base of Round Top westward towards Kern's house on the Emmittsburg road."

3. Captain H. C. Parsons, First Vermont Cavalry, says in *Battles and Leaders of the Civil War*: "I was near Kilpatrick when he impetuously gave the order to Farnsworth to make the last charge. Farnsworth (continued opposite)

The charge was most desperate. The First West Virginia and Eighteenth Pennsylvania moved through the woods first, closely followed by the First Vermont and Fifth New York, and drove the enemy before them until the heavy stone walls and fences were reached. Here the formation was broken; but two regiments cleared the obstacles, charged a second line of infantry, and were again stopped by another stone wall, covering a third line of infantry. One of the supporting cavalry regiments, after passing the first wall, encountered a large body of the enemy which had been sent from the enemy's left to cut off the retreat of the first charging column. The contest became hand-to-hand, and the cavalry used their sabres to such advantage as to disable a great many of their opponents and cause others to surrender. Being exposed to the enemy's artillery and sharpshooters, this regiment was at length obliged to fall back. If even a portion of the Federal infantry posted on Kilpatrick's right had advanced on Law's attenuated line at the time Farnsworth's men had gained the enemy's rear, the Confederate division must have given way. But no cooperation took place. As it was, one of the regiments in the first charging line the First West Virginia after passing the two stone fences already referred to, was entirely surrounded, but succeeded in cutting its way back with a loss of but five killed and four wounded, bringing with it a number of prisoners.

---

spoke with emotion: 'General, do you mean it? Shall I throw my handful of men over rough ground, through timber, against a brigade of infantry? The First Vermont has already been fought half to pieces; these are too good men to kill!' Kilpatrick said: 'Do you refuse to obey my orders? If you are afraid to lead this charge. I will lead it.' Farnsworth rose in his stirrups, looking magnificent in his passion, and cried, 'Take that back!' Kilpatrick returned his defiance, but soon repenting, said: 'I did not mean it; forget it.' For a moment there was silence, when Farnsworth spoke calmly: 'General, if you order the charge, I will lead it, but you must take the responsibility.' I did not hear the low conversation that followed, but as Farnsworth turned away, he said: 'I will obey your order,' Kilpatrick said earnestly: 'I take the responsibility.'"

All things considered it seems wonderful that these four regiments did not suffer a greater percentage of killed, wounded, and missing.[4] It can perhaps, best be accounted for by the moral effect of the charge, and the fine horsemanship with which the fearless troopers leaped the obstacles and sabred the infantrymen in their positions. Of this, the Confederate General Law has said: "It was impossible to use our artillery to any advantage, owing to the close quarters of the attacking cavalry with our own men, the leading squadrons forcing their horses up to the very muzzles of the rifles of our infantry."

---

4. There were 300 men in Farnsworth's charge, and 65 casualties. (Captain Parsons, in *Battles and Leaders of the Civil War*.)

CHAPTER 11

Across the Rappahannock

The Federal victory at the battle of Gettysburg owes much to the cavalry. Buford at Oak Hill, Gregg on the Federal right, and Kilpatrick on the left, performed deeds which have never been excelled by the cavalry of any nation. As Gettysburg was the turning-point in the fortunes of the Union Army, it also marked an epoch in the development of cavalry, trained in methods which were evolved from no foreign text-books, but from stern experience on the battle-fields of the great Civil War.

By the morning of the 4th of July General Lee's lines were evacuated, his army was in full retreat, and the Federal cavalry and the Sixth Army Corps were in hot pursuit, striving to gain his rear, cut his lines of communication, and harass and annoy him in every manner possible.

The First Cavalry Division moved from Westminster to Frederick, where it was joined by the Reserve Brigade under Merritt on July 5th. On the following day it moved towards Williamsport to destroy the enemy's trains, reported to be crossing the Potomac into Virginia. Upon nearing the town the Confederate pickets were driven in until the enemy's line of battle became too strong for further progress. In an attack on Gamble's brigade on the Federal left the enemy was severely punished, but the destruction of the enemy's trains in the face of the strong force guarding them proved too difficult a task for the division, with the exception of a small train of grain with about forty mules.

Meanwhile Kilpatrick's division had marched on July 4th from Gettysburg to Emmittsburg, where it was joined by Huey's brigade of Gregg's division, and from thence it moved towards Monterey, with the intention of destroying the enemy's wagon trains near Hagerstown. After a series of combats with Stuart's cavalry, the Third Division reached Smithburg on July 5th, having entirely destroyed a large wagon train of Ewell's, and having captured 1,360 prisoners, one battle-flag, and a large number of horses and mules.

On July 6th, while Buford was attacking Williamsport, Kilpatrick attacked Stuart at Hagerstown, resulting in that general's surprise and retreat towards Greencastle. Kilpatrick then endeavoured to cooperate with Buford at Williamsport, but failed to gain any material advantage. The enemy, however, was forced to burn a large train north-west of Hagerstown.

From the 7th until the 14th of July, Kilpatrick's division was constantly engaged with the enemy on the right of the Federal army, as was Buford's division on the left, and Huey's brigade of Gregg's division in the centre.

Meanwhile Gregg had followed the enemy by way of Cashtown, where a number of prisoners were captured. The division then proceeded by way of Marion and Chambersburg to Boonesborough; McIntosh's brigade being placed at Emmittsburg to prevent raids of the Confederate cavalry towards the Federal rear.

On July 14th Gregg, with McIntosh's and Irvin Gregg's brigades, crossed the Potomac at Harper's Ferry, and being reinforced by Huey's brigade, marched to Shepherdstown with a view of striking the enemy in flank and rear. On the 16th, Huey's brigade not being present, Gregg was attacked by the enemy in force. After a spirited engagement, lasting all day, the enemy withdrew.

On the same day Buford's and Kilpatrick's divisions followed the enemy closely to Falling Waters, capturing many prisoners, three battle-flags, and a large quantity of stores.

After July 15th the pursuit of the enemy through the London Valley and across the Rappahannock River was made by detachments, and the Gettysburg campaign, so far as the movements of the cavalry corps were concerned, properly closed at that date.

By the end of July the entire cavalry corps was concentrated about Warrenton, Warrenton Junction, and Fayetteville, Virginia, and was again engaged in picketing the Rappahannock. The casualties of the corps from June 28th to July 31st consisted of 1,949 killed, wounded, and missing.

CHAPTER 12

Concerning the Matter of Horses

During the first two years of the war 284,000 horses were furnished the cavalry, when the maximum number of cavalrymen in the field at any time during this period did not exceed 60,000.

The enormous number of casualties among the horses was due to many causes, among which were: ignorance of purchasing officers as to the proper animals for cavalry service; poor horsemanship on the part of the raw cavalry troopers, mustered in at the beginning of the war; the control of the cavalry movements by officers of other arms, ignorant of the limit of endurance of cavalry horses; the hardships inseparable from the duties of the cavalry upon such duties as the Stoneman raid, the campaign of the Army of Virginia, and the campaign of Gettysburg; and last, but not least, ignorance and gross inefficiency on the part of many officers and men as to the condition of the horses backs and feet, care as to food and cleanliness, and the proper treatment of the many diseases to which horses on active service are subject.

Cavalry, of all arms, requires the greatest length of time to acquire efficiency, and if the reduction of the regular establishment of the Army of the United States is ever contemplated, the experience of the Government during these first two years of the War of the Rebellion with horses alone should serve as a warning.

Given men possessing unbounded patriotism, intelligence, and physical excellence, as were the volunteers at the beginning of this war, yet these qualities, while quickly combining to make excellent infantry and artillery soldiers, required many times the length of time to make good cavalrymen. Training and discipline, backed by the unlimited finances of a great government, prevailed in the end; but the lesson, to say the least, was a humiliating and costly one, which should never be repeated.

In such a tremendous machine as the Quartermaster's Department of the Army of the Potomac, containing at the beginning of the war many officers with absolutely no experience as quartermasters, there were necessarily many vexatious delays in purchasing and forwarding supplies, and many disappointments in the quality of supplies, furnished too often by scheming contractors.

The tardiness, too, with which cavalry remounts were forwarded to the regiments was a frequent subject of complaint. In October, 1862, when service in the Peninsular campaign and that of the Army of Virginia had brought the numbers of mounted cavalry down to less than a good-sized regiment, General McClellan wrote to Halleck: "It is absolutely necessary that some energetic measures be taken to supply the cavalry of this army with remount horses. The present rate of supply is 1,050 per week for the entire army here and in front of Washington. From this number the artillery draw for their batteries."

In reply to this the quartermaster-general stated that since the battles in front of Washington there had been issued to the Army, to replace losses, 9,254 horses, adding: "Is there an instance on record of such a drain and destruction of horses in a country not a desert?" A little later McClellan again complained that many of the horses furnished "were totally unfitted for the service, and should never have been received." General Pope had, in fact, reported that "our cavalry numbered on paper about 4,000 men, but their horses were completely broken down, and there were not 500 men, all told, capable of doing much service, as should be expected from cavalry. On the morning of the 30th [August 30, 1862], the artillery and cavalry horses had been saddled and in harness for ten days, and had had no forage for two days previous." And again he says: "Our cavalry at Centerville was completely broken down, no horses whatever having reached us to remount it. Generals Buford and Bayard, commanding the whole of the cavalry force of the Army, reported to me that there were not five horses to the company that could be forced into a trot."

The demand for horses was so great that in many cases they were sent on active service before recovering sufficiently from the fatigue incident to a long railway journey. One case was reported of horses left on the cars fifty hours without food or water, and then being taken out, issued, and used for immediate service.[1]

To such an extent had overwork and disease reduced the number of cavalry horses that when General Stuart made his raid into Pennsylvania October 11. 1862, only 800 Federal cavalry could be mounted to follow him, and the exhausting pursuit which took place broke down a large proportion of the horses that remained. Under date of October 21st, McClellan wrote to Halleck: "Exclusive of the cavalry force now engaged in picketing the river, I have not at present over 1,000 horses for service. Without more cavalry horses, our communications from the moment we march would be at the mercy of the large cavalry force of the enemy."

---

1. General Meigs report, *Rebellion Records,* Vol. 19., Part 1., page 19.

The need of cavalry was so urgent and the numbers of dismounted men so alarming that even President Lincoln wrote to McClellan, October 27, 1862: "To be told, after five weeks total inaction of the Army, during which time we have sent to the Army every fresh horse we possibly could, amounting on the whole to 7,918, that the cavalry horses were too much fatigued to move, presents a cheerless, almost hopeless prospect for the future."

The reorganization of the cavalry under Hooker worked a great improvement in the care and condition of horses, as it tended to systematize the forwarding of remounts, and by a centralization of authority brought the whole cavalry force under a stricter sense of responsibility for casualties among the hordes. It also reduced the excessive picket duty, which many corps and division commanders had deemed the chief duty of cavalry. But little by little officers and men were beginning to realize how important the health and strength of their chargers were to them, and by actual experience on many arduous campaigns they were gradually learning how best to preserve that health and strength.

But the Stoneman raid again necessarily reduced the numbers of serviceable horses. Stoneman reported that while the horses were generally in fair condition when they started, they were much exhausted and weakened by the march. Many were rendered temporarily useless from infrequent feeding, "mud fever," and sore backs, while at least a thousand were abandoned. Numbers of men thus dismounted procured remounts from the country, mostly brood-mares and draught-horses, which, though unsuitable for cavalry service, served for temporary use.

This raid, followed by the battle of Beverly Ford, was a poor preparation, so far as horse-flesh was concerned, for the Gettysburg campaign which followed. In immediate readiness for action, constantly in motion night and day, saddled for long periods,[2] fed and groomed at irregular times, often unshod in a country from which the Confederate cavalry had collected every horse-shoe, the horses of the Union cavalry fought their battles of the Gettysburg campaign at a disadvantage. Had not the enemy's cavalry been in much the same condition, this would have been a serious consideration.

Aside, too, from the ordinary diseases to which horses are subject, the Virginia soil seemed to be particularly productive of diseases of the feet. That known as "scratches" disabled thousands of horses during the Peninsular campaign and that of Pope, and late in 1863, after the Bristoe campaign, General Merritt reported: "Since arriving in camp I have sent to the Quartermaster's Department, Washington City, according to order, 471 disabled, unserviceable horses. There are at least 100 more in the command. This leaves the entire strength for duty not more than 1,500. The frightful loss among horses is owing to a disease which resembles tetter (called in the Army, foot-rot), from the effects of which the finest appearing horses in the command became disabled in one day s march. The disease seems to have been contracted in the quartermaster corrals, in Washington."

Such was the enormous expense of the cavalry arm of the service during the first two years of the war that in July, 1863, the Cavalry Bureau was established. The order of the Secretary of War relative to its establishment contained the following: "The enormous expense attending the maintenance of the cavalry arm points to the necessity of greater care and more judicious management on the part of cavalry officers, that their horses may be constantly kept up to the standard of efficiency for service. Great neglects of duty in this connection are to be attributed to officers in command

2. From Warrenton Junction to Thoroughfare Gap, the horses were not unsaddled for two days.

of cavalry troops. It is the design of the War Department to correct such neglects by dismissing from service officers whose inefficiency and inattention result in the deterioration and loss of the public animals under their charge."

The Cavalry Bureau was charged with the organization and equipment of the cavalry forces. It further more provided that the mounts and remounts be purchased and inspected under its direction, by officers of the Quartermaster's Department and cavalry service, respectively.

Depôts were established at important cities one of the principal depôts being at Giesboro Point, near Washington. The establishment of a "dismounted camp," near Washington, where cavalrymen were sent to be refitted, worked great injury to the cavalry service, as the men purposely lost their equipments and neglected their horses for the purpose of being sent to the "dismounted camp." So pernicious had been the effect of this camp that on October 26th General Meade recommended that all horses, arms, and equipments for the dismounted men be sent out to the army as needed.

The first chief of the Cavalry Bureau was General Stoneman, followed January 2, 1864, by General Garrard; he in turn being succeeded in the 26th of the same month by General J. H. Wilson. On the 14th of April, 1864, it was directed that the Cavalry Bureau be under charge of the chief of army staff; the duties pertaining to organization, equipment, and inspection of cavalry being performed by a cavalry officer, while those of the purchase, inspection, subsistence, and transportation of horses were performed by an officer of the Quartermaster's Department.

The establishment of this bureau worked a decided improvement in the supply system of the mounted aim and much of the success of the Federal cavalry is to be attributed to the systematic and efficient manner in which the officers of the bureau performed their duties. That it was difficult for even the Cavalry Bureau to keep the supply of remounts up to the number required, is shown from the fact that General Sheridan states in his *Memoirs* that "only 1,900 horses were furnished the Army of the Potomac from April 6 to August 14, 1864 not enough to meet casualties and that it was necessary for him to send his dismounted men into camp."

CHAPTER 13

Culpeper Court House

The months of August and September were marked by several important reconnaissances by the cavalry.[1]

On August 1st General Buford advanced from Rapidan Station with his cavalry division and drove the enemy's, cavalry towards Culpeper Court House. The enemy's infantry caused the division to retire, but the reconnaissance had the effect of causing Lee to draw his infantry south of the Rapidan. Towards the end of this month regiments of the Second Cavalry Division engaged the enemy at Edwards Ferry, Hartwood Church, Barbee's Cross-Roads, and Rixey's Ford.

Again, on September 1st, General Kilpatrick with the Third Cavalry Division marched to Port Conway on the lower Rappahannock, where he drove a force of the enemy's cavalry across the river and, with his artillery, destroyed the gunboats *Reliance* and *Satellite*.

Another cavalry fight took place September 13th to 17th. It had been reported that the enemy was making a retrograde movement, and General Pleasanton with all the

---

1. On the 15th of August the Reserve Brigade was ordered to Giesboro Point to refit. On August 12th the Second Brigade, Second Cavalry Division, was broken up; the Second New York going to the First Brigade, Third Division; the Fourth New York to the Second Brigade, First Division; and the First Rhode Island, Sixth Ohio, and Eighth Pennsylvania to the two remaining brigades of the Second Cavalry Division.

cavalry, supported by the Second Army Corps under General Warren, crossed the river at a number of points, driving the enemy's cavalry across the Rapidan, and capturing three guns and a number of prisoners. The fords of the Rapidan were found fortified and held by such strong bodies of the enemy's infantry as to prevent the cavalry from crossing.

On September 16th the Army of the Potomac crossed the Rappahannock and took position near Culpeper Court House, with two corps advanced to the Rapidan. The fords on the latter river were found to be too strongly guarded to be forced. Just as a flank movement had been matured, the Eleventh and Twelfth Army Corps were withdrawn from the Army of the Potomac, for duty in the Southwest.

During the next few weeks the cavalry was actively engaged in reconnoitering duty. On September 21st Buford and Kilpatrick crossed the Rapidan, their purpose being to develop the enemy's strength and position about his left flank. Stuart's cavalry was encountered and driven back, and the fact that two of the enemy's infantry corps were north of Gordonsville was discovered.

Information having been received that the enemy was about to make some important movement, General Buford was, on October 10th, sent across the Rapidan with the First Cavalry Division, to uncover, if possible, the upper fords of the river, while the First and Sixth Army Corps would attempt to force the fords in their front.

On this same day, before any word had been received from Buford, the enemy crossed the Robertson River, and advanced in heavy force from the direction of Madison Court House, driving in the Federal cavalry. As there was every indication that this force was endeavouring to pass the flank of the Union army, General Meade, on the following day (October 11th), withdrew his army to the north bank of the Rappahannock.

Meanwhile Buford had forced a passage over the; Germanna Ford, although without a pound of forage for his horses. He then proceeded along the river, capturing the enemy's pickets at the fords, and bivouacking that night at Morton's Ford. As the First Division train had in the meantime been ordered to recross the river, and the First Army Corps had retired, Buford was at a loss to know just what to do, especially as the enemy was pressing him hard. He finally recrossed the Rapidan at Morton's Ford and engaged a body of the enemy that had crossed at the Raccoon Ford. Finally learning that General Pleasanton with the Third Cavalry Division was still in the rear of the Third Army Corps, Buford determined to hold his position until the arrival of that division. The next day the First Division, with Sedgwick's corps, made a reconnaissance in force to Brandy Station, and accomplished its purpose of discovering the enemy s strength and position.

Meanwhile the Second Cavalry Division had proceeded from Culpeper Court House on the 11th instant to Sulphur Springs, with orders to feel the enemy towards Sperryville and Little Washington. This was successfully accomplished, but the division was compelled by superior numbers to recross to the east side of the river. As the enemy advanced, the cavalry fell slowly back to Auburn, covering the rear of the Second Army Corps.

At daylight on the 14th instant the enemy attacked Gregg's division, but he held his position tenaciously, while General Warren got the Second Corps across Cedar Run. After this stubborn contest the cavalry fell back slowly, and after dark moved to Brentsville to assist General Buford with the wagon trains. During this arduous rear-guard duty, the First Maine Cavalry, which had been cut oft in its return from Sperryville, made a circuitous march of ninety miles, and reported in safety at Bristoe Station.

The Third Cavalry Division was, at the beginning of the enemy's movement across the Rapidan, picketing from Griffinsburg near Hazel Run, through Russell's Ford on Robertson's River to the vicinity of James City.

On the 10th of October the enemy moved through Cregler's Mills, Russell's Ford, and Creglersville, and, although its advance of artillery and cavalry presented a bold front, the Third Cavalry Division succeeded in holding its position throughout the day. At 3 o'clock in the morning of the following day, the division received orders — in keeping with the general withdrawal of the Army of the Potomac to fall back to Culpeper Court House, covering the rear of the Third and Fifth Army Corps. As the enemy approached Culpeper, Pennington's battery opened upon them from the hills north of the town, and the entire cavalry division fell back on Brandy Station. Here it was found that the enemy had taken up a position immediately in front of the division, and was also approaching the left flank. The command was accordingly massed in column of squadrons. General Davies having the right and General Custer the left. A charge of a large force of the enemy's cavalry was met and broken by a counter-charge, and the division continuing to advance in good order, the enemy broke and fled in great confusion. Passing on, Kilpatrick effected a junction with Buford's division, and crossed the Rappahannock about 8 o'clock in the evening. On the morning of the 12th, the division moved to Fayetteville to reinforce General Gregg, and from there moved through Buckland Mills, encamping on the 13th at Sudley Springs.

On the 15th, the Army of the Potomac remained in position at Centerville, with skirmishing at Blackburn's Ford and at Liberty Mills; and on the 17th the enemy made a further attempt to turn the right flank of the army, retiring again on the 18th.

On the 19th, with the Third Cavalry Division in advance, the army moved to Gainesville. On the 20th the Third Division moved out on the Warrenton Pike, driving the enemy from Gainesville and across Broad Run. Davies brigade advanced from Buckland Mills to New Baltimore, where it narrowly escaped being cut off by a column of the enemy's cavalry and infantry, advancing from the direction of Auburn. The Seventh Michigan was sent out to delay the enemy. Custer's brigade formed line of battle, and Davies' brigade was ordered to retire. The Michigan regiment was driven in on Custer, whose skirmish line repulsed the Confederate cavalry, but under stress of superior numbers was forced to retire.

Davies brigade was at this time slowly retiring, and Custer crossed Broad Run and took up a position. enabling Davies to cross safely by the right of the town, the enemy not being able to attack him with out passing within range of Custer's artillery. Custer then fell back upon the infantry supports at Gainesville, and Davies extricated himself by marching to New Market.

On the 20th instant the Army of the Potomac again occupied Warrenton, the enemy retiring to the south bank of the Rappahannock, having destroyed the Orange & Alexandria Railroad from Bristoe Station to the Rappahannock, and by the 22nd both armies were again recuperating in camp.

In the arduous work of the cavalry corps as advance and rear guard during the Bristoe campaign, October 9th to 22nd, it suffered a total of 1,251 casualties, which included four officers killed and twenty-nine wounded.[2]

---

2. That this highly efficient work of the cavalry was not duly appreciated is shown from the fact that in congratulatory General Orders No. 96, of October 15, 1863, the cavalry was not mentioned. General Gregg accordingly asked for either a court of inquiry upon his conduct as commander of the Second Cavalry Division, or that he be relieved at once from command. In replying, General Meade disclaimed any intention (continued overleaf)

But the period of rest did not last long. General Meade submitted to the general-in-chief a plan for the seizure of the heights above Fredericksburg, thus transferring the base of operations to the Fredericksburg Railroad. This plan not being approved, it was decided to force the passage of the Rappahannock.

Accordingly, on November 7th General Sedgwick advanced to Rappahannock Station with the Fifth and Sixth Army Corps, finding the enemy strongly in trenched on the north bank of the river. General French, with the First, Second, and Third Army Corps, marched to Kelly's Ford.

Sedgwick attacked and carried the enemy's works on the north bank, capturing four pieces of artillery and 1,600 prisoners; and the Third Corps of French's command likewise gallantly forced the passage of the river at Kelly's Ford.

During these operations the First Cavalry Division under Buford moved on the right flank, crossing at the upper fords and forcing the passage of Hazel River at Rixeyville, thus cooperating with Sedgwick.

Kilpatrick's division operated similarly on the left flank, crossing the river at Ellis Ford, and cooperating with French's left infantry column. Gregg's division was held in reserve, guarding the trains at Bealeton and Morrisville.

The cavalry took part in the pursuit of the enemy to Brandy Station, and as far as Culpeper. The Army of the Potomac then took position from Kelly's Ford through Brandy Station to Welford's Ford; and the work of repairing the Orange & Alexandria Railroad to the Rappahannock was begun immediately. By the 16th of November the railroad and a bridge over the Rappahannock was completed; and by the 19th sidings and a depot at Brandy Station, where supplies for the army were brought forward and delivered.

of disparaging the services of the cavalry, and in General Order No. 97, following, bore testimony to "the activity, zeal, and gallantry" of the whole cavalry corps during the operations from the Rapidan to Centerville.

CHAPTER 14

The Raid on Richmond

By the end of November the Army of the Potomac was ready for another advance southward. A front attack was deemed impracticable, as the position of the enemy along the Rapidan was strongly entrenched. Preparations were accordingly made for an advance on the enemy's flank. On November 26th the Federal army crossed the Rapidan in three columns at Jacobs , Germanna, and Culpeper Fords. The Third Corps (French's) crossed at Jacob's Ford, followed by the Sixth Corps (Sedgwicks'); the Second Corps (Warren's) crossed at Germanna Ford; and the Fifth Corps (Sykes') crossed at Culpeper Ford, followed by the First Corps (Newton's).

Gregg's division was ordered to operate on the left flank of the army, Buford's[1] on the right, to cover the movement, and Kilpatrick's to hold the fords of the Rapidan until further orders. Detachments of cavalry, each hundred strong, were also ordered to report to Generals French, Sykes, and Warren, commanding the advanced corps.

---

1. In November General Buford was permitted to go to Washington for surgical treatment, and during the Mine Run campaign General Wesley Merritt commanded the First Cavalry Division, and Colonel Alfred Gibbs the Reserve Brigade General Buford had been wounded, and his constant work in the field had told severely upon his constitution. In Washington he gradually grew worse, and on December 16, 1863 the very day that the President signed his commission as major-general he died, the *beau* ideal of a cavalry officer, on the threshold of a still more brilliant career.

Gregg's division crossed the Rappahannock at Ellis' Ford on the 24th instant, and proceeded to Ely's Ford on the Rapidan. The advance guard crossed and took possession of the heights, but later the entire division was withdrawn to Richardsville and Ellis' Ford. On the 26th the division crossed the Rapidan, and operated in the direction of the head waters of the Po River. On the 27th it passed through Parker's Store, and took position on the Orange plank road, in advance of the Fifth Army Corps. At New Hope Meeting House, the enemy's skirmishers were encountered and driven back with loss by three of the advance regiments of the division. The cavalry division's casualties this day were 106.

On the 30th Devin's brigade of this division, which had been protecting the wagon trains of the army, joined Gregg's division, and was posted at the Wilderness. The First Brigade moved to Parker's Store.

Meanwhile the Third Cavalry Division, under Custer, had, on the 26th instant, left camp near Stevensburg, and moved to the Rapidan River, Davies brigade taking position near Raccoon Ford, and Town's brigade at Morton's Ford. The First West Virginia Cavalry was sent to guard the fords between Germanna and Morton's; and the Sixth Michigan to Somerville Ford, to patrol that and adjacent fords. Custer's instructions required him to make demonstrations as if to cross from Morton's Ford upwards, the moment he heard cannonading below. This he did, as soon as he heard the artillery, and succeeded in drawing the fire of thirty of the enemy's guns upon his force, accompanied by the moving forward of a large body of the enemy's infantry. The demonstration was highly successful, and kept two entire divisions (Rode's and Early's) of Ewell's corps standing to arms all night. But in the morning of the 27th, having discovered the intentions of the Federal army, the Confederate infantry and artillery between Morton's and Raccoon fords was withdrawn.

The Second Brigade of this cavalry division accordingly crossed the river, and, occupying the enemy's entrenchments, drove their cavalry back several miles. During the remainder of the day and the following day skirmishing occurred with the enemy's cavalry, and during the next five days the command merely watched the fords.

The campaign was a failure, so far as flanking the enemy's position was concerned, General Meade attributing it to the fact that the Third Corps (French's), through taking the wrong road, was so slow moving out to Robertson's Tavern on the 27th inst. that the other corps became engaged before the Third was within supporting distance. The enemy was so strongly entrenched that, rather than risk an assault on their works, it was decided to again fall back behind the Rapidan.

This was accomplished on the night of December 1st, the army's movements being covered by the Second Cavalry Division, Devin's brigade of the First Division, and two brigades of infantry from the Third Army Corps, the whole under the command of General Gregg.

Again had the Army of the Potomac retired with out effecting its object. Winter was at hand, and the troops went into winter quarters. Early in January the Government offered a furlough and agreed to pay a bounty to soldiers who would re-enlist for three years. A large number of cavalrymen did so, and were sent home on furlough.

The cavalry troops in winter quarters made them selves as comfortable as their surroundings permitted, but their anticipated rest from active duty hardly materialized. In addition to the fatiguing picket and outpost duty, there were continual scouts, reconnaissances, and several raids, to keep the cavalry busy, while the infantry was recuperating for the spring campaign.

And here it may be proper to say that General Hooker's original plan of consolidating the cavalry and giving its leader independence of action had not been completely realized. The ever-present outpost duty still continued, and this, with continual detached service on minor reconnaissances, guarding wagon trains, could not but result in a lack of unity in the cavalry corps.

Late in December, the Second, Eighth, and Sixteenth Pennsylvania and First Maine Cavalry regiments, under the command of Colonel Charles H. Smith, marched from Bealeton to Luray, Virginia, surprising a number of small detachments of the enemy and capturing a number of prisoners. At Luray they destroyed a large amount of property useful to the Confederate Government, and returned in safety, having marched one hundred miles without a single casualty.

Early in January, Fitzhugh Lee, with a large cavalry command, invaded Hampshire and Hardy counties, West Virginia. General Kelly, commanding the Department of West Virginia, confronted the enemy with all his available force; after destroying a number of wagons and securing such supplies as he could find. Lee's command withdrew, having suffered severely from the intensely cold weather. Later in the month these same counties were subject to another raid by General Early, in which the cavalry forces of West Virginia, the First New York, the Fifteenth New York, the Twenty-first New York, Cole's (Maryland) Cavalry, and detachments of the Second Maryland, Sixth Michigan, and First Connecticut Cavalry were engaged. The main object of the enemy, the capture of the garrison at Petersburg and the destruction of the Baltimore & Ohio Railroad, was successful; but the Confederate General Rosser succeeded in capturing a large wagon train.

The hampering of the cavalry by orders from the infantry officer commanding the infantry supports and the great difficulty of successfully concentrating troops in so rough a country contributed to the safe withdrawal of the enemy's forces.

Although a number of minor engagements occurred during the month of January, nothing of great importance took place until February 6th, when a demonstration was made along the Rapidan, participated in by the First and Second Army Corps and the First and Third Cavalry Divisions.

While the infantry was engaging the enemy at Morton's and Raccoon fords, the First Cavalry Division (Merritt's) crossed the Robertson River in two columns, at Smoot's and Ayler's Fords; and the Third Cavalry Division (Kilpatrick's) crossed at Culpeper, Ely's, and Germanna Fords.

On the 7th the First Cavalry Division moved to Barnett's Ford, and brisk skirmishing ensued. The demonstration on this ford continued until about 1 o'clock p. m., resulting in the deployment of a Confederate infantry brigade. The Third Cavalry Division reconnoitered in all directions, after crossing the Rapidan, finding the enemy in much the same position as during the preceding November.

During this month the cavalry was greatly annoyed by guerrillas, a large number of small detachments being ambushed and either shot down or captured. So serious did these losses become that a general order was issued, threatening with court-martial officers and men who allowed themselves to be surprised and captured while on duty. West Virginia and western Virginia suffered greatly from these irregular marauding forces, and on February 11th Gilmore's guerrillas threw a Baltimore & Ohio express train from the track at Kearneysville and robbed the passengers. And on February 20th, in an attempt to capture the noted Major Mosby at Upperville and Front Royal, a severe skirmish took place between Mosby's command and a portion of the cavalry brigade of the Department of West Virginia.

On the 28th of February Custer's cavalry division undertook a raid into Albemarle County, Virginia. The command marched by way of Madison Court House and Standardsville without opposition and took the road to Charlottesville, where Fitzhugh Lee's force was in camp. The division approached within three miles of the place, when, finding the enemy in superior numbers, Custer withdrew, burning the bridges over the Rivanna River and destroying much property. Near Standardsville his force having been reduced to 1,000 men through a misunderstanding, by which a portion of the command had marched beyond the Rapidan, he was charged by the First and Fifth Virginia Cavalry, led by General Stuart in person. The charge threw the advance guard one squadron of the Fifth United States Cavalry back upon the main body; but the entire regiment, charging forward, drove the enemy back in great disorder. Custer pursued with his whole command to Bank's Ford, and then, wheeling about, eluded the enemy, who had concentrated here, by moving rapidly to the ford and crossing. The command marched 150 miles, captured one battle-standard, fifty prisoners, 500 horses, and six caissons, and destroyed an immense amount of property.

This raid was made to distract attention from an other raid of greater proportions, begun the same day by General Kilpatrick, and having as its object the taking of the city of Richmond and the liberation of the Union prisoners confined there. Incidentally, the President's proclamation of amnesty was to be distributed throughout the hostile territory.

It had been learned that Richmond was, about this time, comparatively defenceless, and it was thought that, by a rapid and secret march, the city might be captured and the prisoners released before reinforcements from either Petersburg or Lee's army could reach there.

General Kilpatrick left his camp at Stevensburg at 7 o'clock p. m., February 28th, with 3,595 picked men and Ransom's horse battery. The advance, consisting of 460 men under Colonel Ulric Dahlgren, crossed at Ely's Ford, capturing the enemy's picket. Then, leaving the main body, it proceeded through Spottsylvania Court House to Frederick's Hall, where it captured a Confederate general court-martial, consisting of 13 officers. It then proceeded through dense woods and swamps to the James River, which it reached about 7 a. m. on March 2nd. having destroyed considerable Confederate property *en route*. But through the alleged treachery of a guide the little command had been led out of its course, and instead of being near Richmond, the latter was still eighteen miles away. However, Dahlgren continued his march and even passed the outer line of the city's works, when he was attacked from both sides of the road and from the front. A desperate fight followed. Colonel Dahlgren with about 150 men pushed on, hoping to get through the Confederate lines by way of the James River; but about midnight the command fell into an ambuscade; Dahlgren was killed, together with a number of his men, and the remainder captured. The other part of Dahlgren's force under Captain Mitchell, Second New York Cavalry, succeeded finally in joining Kilpatrick at Tunstall's Station, with forty-four casualties.

Meanwhile Kilpatrick, after passing through Spottsylvania Court House, had taken a south-easterly course, crossed the South Anna at Ground Squirrel Bridge, and reached the outer line of works about Richmond without serious opposition. The first line of defence was successfully passed, and preparations were made to assault the main works; but nothing having been heard from Dahlgren's party, which was to have made a simultaneous attack from the other side, and the enemy being heavily reinforced, Kilpatrick deemed it prudent to retire.

Kilpatrick's attack was made some three hours earlier than Dahlgren's, owing to the latter's delay in reaching Richmond, and thus the Confederates were prepared to meet Dahlgren when he finally reached their works.

Kilpatrick withdrew across the Chickahominy and succeeded in reaching General Butler's lines on the Peninsula March 3rd.

As its commander afterwards reported: "The expedition failed in its great object, but through no fault of the officers and men accompanying it. All did their duty bravely, promptly, and well, for which they deserve the highest praise. Considerable property was destroyed, and several thousand of the President's proclamations scattered through the country. If Colonel Dahlgren had not failed in crossing the river, which he did either through the ignorance or treachery of his guide, or had the enemy at Bottom's Bridge been forced to remain at that point by a threatened attack from the direction of Yorktown, I should have entered the rebel capital and released our prisoners."

Confirmatory of this opinion, a letter written by General Wade Hampton to General Stuart, March 6th, contained the following: "My observations convinced me that the enemy could have taken Richmond, and in all probability would have done so but for the fact that Colonel Johnson intercepted a dispatch from Dahlgren to Kilpatrick, asking what hour the latter had fixed for an attack on the city, so that both attacks might be simultaneous."

As part reprisal for the killing of Dahlgren, General Butler on March 9th sent an expedition consisting of a brigade of infantry and about 700 of Kilpatrick's cavalry to

King and Queen counties. There they drove the Fifth and Ninth Virginia Cavalry from their camp, burned the latter with much Confederate property, and took a number of prisoners.

CHAPTER 15

Grant, Sheridan & Spottsylvania

During the winter many changes important to the cavalry as well as to the entire army had taken place.

On the 12th of March Lieutenant-General Ulysses S. Grant had been assigned to command the armies of the United States, with General Halleck as chief-of- staff in Washington. And on the 25th of the same month General Pleasanton was relieved from command of the cavalry corps, General Gregg taking temporary command, and was superseded on April 4th by Major-General Philip H. Sheridan.

General A. T. A. Torbert was placed in command of the First Cavalry Division, his brigade commanders being Custer and Devin, with Merritt in command of the Reserve Brigade. The Second Cavalry Division remained in command of General Gregg, with Davies and Irvin Gregg as brigade commanders. The Third Cavalry Division was assigned to General James H. Wilson, with Colonels Bryan and Chapman as brigade commanders.

Sheridan found the horses of the cavalry corps much run down, and one of the first and most important things that he did was to impress upon General Meade the wastefulness of rendering unserviceable so many thousand horses by unnecessary picket duty, "covering a distance on a continuous line of nearly sixty miles, with hardly a mounted Confederate confronting it at any point." Sheridan also insisted that the cavalry should be concentrated to fight the enemy's cavalry. Meade expressed the traditional views of army commanders, when, in reply, he failed to see who would protect the flanks of the army, the fronts of moving infantry columns, and the wagon trains, if the cavalry were concentrated.

Although Meade promptly relieved the cavalry from much of the arduous picket duty it was performing, he gave little encouragement at the time to Sheridan's plans for an independent cavalry corps a corps in fact as well as in name. But the corps commander bided his time, confident that an opportunity would at length come for the realization of his views. The opportunity came quickly enough.

On May 4th the Army of the Potomac again moved against the Army of Northern Virginia, then occupying an entrenched position south of the Rapidan. General Grant planned, by moving by the left flank, to compel Lee to come out from his entrenchments along Mine Run; and although a serious consideration was the wooded country of the Wilderness, through which he must pass, the manoeuvre had the advantages of using Brandy Station as a base of supplies, and at the same time of covering Washington.

Sheridan had in the neighbourhood of 10,000 cavalry.[1] Gregg's and Wilson's divisions took the advance by way of Ely's and Germanna fords, preceding the Second and Fifth Army Corps respectively, while Torbert's division remained in rear to cover the trains and reserve artillery.

On the 5th Wilson's division advanced from Parker's Store to Craig's Meeting House, where he met the enemy's advance, and, although at first successful, he finally withdrew, for lack of ammunition, to Todd's Tavern, where he formed a junction with Gregg's division. The combined cavalry then drove the enemy back to Shady Grove Church, and

---

1. For the organization of the cavalry May 5th, see Appendix 12.

Sheridan so disposed the force as to hold the Brock road beyond the Furnaces and around through Todd's Tavern to Piney Branch Church.

But on the 6th, although Custer had defeated the enemy at the Furnaces, Meade became alarmed for the safety of his left flank, and ordered Sheridan to withdraw the advanced cavalry towards Chancellorsville, abandoning a position that was to be regained later at heavy cost to both infantry and cavalry.

That Sheridan chafed under this order is seen from his letter to General Humphreys of May 5th: "Why cannot infantry," he says, "be sent to guard the trains, and let me take the offensive?"

On the 7th the army advanced with a view to taking Spottsylvania Court House, and the trains were moved towards Piney Branch Church, now, unknown to Meade, held by the enemy. This led to the battle of Todd's Tavern between Hampton's and Fitzhugh Lee's commands of Stuart's cavalry (about 8,000 men) and Gregg's division, assisted by two brigades of Torbert's division.[2] Irvin Gregg's brigade attacked the enemy on the Catharpen road, Merritt's Reserve Brigade on the Spottsylvania road, and Davies' brigade on the Piney Branch road, uniting with Merritt's left. After severe fighting, in which the enemy showed the greatest resistance in Merritt's front, the Confederates gave way and were pursued almost to Spottsylvania Court House.

In keeping with Grant's purpose of threatening Lee's communications by moving the army to Spottsylvania Court House, Sheridan directed Gregg and Merritt to gain possession of Snell's Bridge, early on the 8th, while Wilson was ordered to take possession of Spottsylvania Court House, and actually reached and held that place till directed

---

2. Torbert was taken ill on the 6th instant, and the command of his division devolved on General Merritt the following day.

to fall back from it. Meade had so amended Sheridan's orders as to direct Gregg to simply hold the Corbin Bridge, and Merritt to act as advance guard for the advancing column of infantry. Had Sheridan's order not been thus modified, it is quite probable that the cavalry would have to delayed the march of the Confederates, who held on to Spottsylvania Court House, till the Federal infantry had advanced and made good their possession of that place. As it was, the enemy had time to fortify the latter place, and the bloody battle of Spottsylvania Court House was fought while the work of the cavalry was practically ineffective.

Sheridan's unwillingness to use his cavalry in this disjointed manner, coupled with additional distaste that Merritt's division should have been accused of delaying the march of the Fifth Army Corps, led to that famous interview between Meade and Sheridan, in which the latter told his senior that he could whip Stuart if allowed to do so, and that henceforth Meade could command the cavalry corps himself, as he (Sheridan) would not give it another order.

General Grant determined that Sheridan should be granted his opportunity to "whip Stuart," and that very day Meade directed that the cavalry be concentrated immediately, and that Sheridan proceed against the enemy's cavalry. When his supplies were exhausted, he was to proceed to Haxall's Landing on the James River, communicating with General Butler.

The country between Spottsylvania and Richmond had been stripped of supplies of all kinds. For this reason, and in order to obtain greater room for cavalry operations, secure from interference from the enemy's infantry, Sheridan decided to march his command south of the North Anna before offering battle.

Mobilized at Aldrich's, the expedition started on the morning of May 9th, and with a column thirteen miles long, Sheridan succeeded in passing at a walk around the right of Lee's army without discovery. The Ny, Po, and Ta rivers were safely passed, and the North Anna reached on the same day; Stuart's cavalry, which followed, being repeatedly held in check by Davies' brigade, which acted as rear guard. Custer's brigade pushed on to Beaver Dam Station to cut the Virginia Central Railroad.

On the day following, the 10th, Gregg's and Wilson's divisions crossed the North Anna, covered while crossing by Merritt's division, which had crossed the preceding day. The cavalry corps then proceeded leisurely by the Negro-foot Road towards Richmond, Stuart meanwhile urging his forces forward, in an endeavour to interpose between the Federal cavalry and the capital of the Confederacy. On the 11th instant Stuart held Yellow Tavern on the Brook Turnpike.

Early in the morning of this day Davies proceeded to Ashland and cut the Fredericksburg Railroad, which so deceived Stuart as to Sheridan's future movements that he divided his forces, Gordon's brigade following the Federal troops and the remainder marching to Yellow Tavern. But Merritt's brigade, having entered the place, drove the enemy back and secured possession of the turnpike. The other Federal divisions being brought up, Custer, with his own brigade, supported by Chapman's brigade of Wilson's division, made a mounted charge on the enemy's left, capturing two guns and breaking their line. Then, while Gibbs and Devin forced the enemy's centre and right, Gregg charged in rear and the battle was won.

This engagement gave Sheridan complete control of the road to Richmond. The casualties on both sides were quite severe, but the Confederate loss included Generals Stuart and James B. Gordon.

Finding the road planted with torpedoes, and there being no road between the enemy's works and the Chickahominy, Sheridan gave up the attempt and crossed to the north side of that river by the Meadow Bridge. This bridge was repaired, under severe fire, by Merritt's brigade, which afterwards pursued the enemy to dairies Mill. But while the bridge was being repaired, the Confederates advanced from their entrenchments with a brigade of infantry and large numbers of dismounted cavalry, while Gordon's cavalry threatened Sheridan along the Brook Road. After a severe contest, the enemy was repulsed and the infantry driven within the works.

On the afternoon of the 12th the Cavalry Corps encamped at Walnut Grove and Gaines Mill; on the 13th at Bottom's Ridge; on the 14th it passed through White Oak Swamp and encamped between Maxall's Landing and Shirley on the James River, and resting there until the 17th, the return march was begun. Proceeding by way of Baltimore Cross-Roads, Sheridan crossed the Pamunkey at White House, repairing the partly destroyed railroad bridge; and then, by way of Aylett's, he rejoined the Army of the Potomac near Chesterfield on the 24th instant.

The raid had accomplished important results. It had materially affected Lee's retrograde movements; had drawn oft Stuart's cavalry, and thus increased the ease of movement of the immense trains of the Army of the Potomac; had brought signal defeat to the Confederate cavalry; had seriously threatened Richmond, and might have taken it; had cut the railroads which connected Lee with Richmond, and had destroyed immense quantities of stores which, with the strained resources of the Confederacy at this time, must, no doubt, have exerted a powerful influence on the result of the war.

CHAPTER 16

Hanover Court House to Petersburg

Spottsylvania's battles had been fought when Sheridan returned, and the Army of the Potomac was manoeuvring to cross the North Anna.

On the 25th instant Wilson's cavalry division was ordered to make a reconnaissance across this river as far as Little Elver; and from the 26th to the 30th the division was engaged in this duty, at the same time covering the right flank of the army. On the 31st Wilson crossed the south side of the Pamunkey, defeating a division of the enemy's cavalry under W. H. F. Lee. Pushing on the same day, in accordance with an order from General Meade, Wilson occupied Hanover Court House, after a sharp fight, in which the Confederate General P. M. B. Young was wounded; and on the following day, June 1st, destroyed the bridges over the South Anna. Simultaneously therewith he had a sharp engagement with the Confederate cavalry, but the latter being reinforced by infantry, and Wilson having accomplished the object of his movement, he withdrew by the head of the Totopotomy to Hawes' Shop, where he again came within supporting distance of the army. Meanwhile Gregg's and Torbert's divisions, supported by Russell's division of the Sixth Corps, were covering the crossing of the army over the Pamunkey. In effecting this crossing,

Gregg made a feint of crossing at Littlepage's and Torbert at Taylor's Ford. Both then, after dark, discreetly retired, and successfully crossed at Hanovertown Ford on the 27th, Custer's brigade in the lead. Pushing rapidly on to Hanovertown, Torbert is division encountered Gordon's brigade of Confederate cavalry, and drove it in confusion in the direction of Hanover Court House. Gregg's division moved up to this line; Russell's division of infantry encamped near the river crossing, in support, and behind the screen thus formed the Army of the Potomac crossed the river on the 28th instant unimpeded.

As General Grant was now uncertain of Lee's exact position, Gregg was ordered to reconnoitre towards Mechanicsville. At Hawes' Shop he found confronting him Hampton's and Fitzhugh Lee's cavalry divisions,[2] supported by Butler's cavalry brigade, and he attacked them dismounted at once. The fight which followed was very severe, and continued late into the evening, as the position contended for was one of great strategic importance to both armies. Custer's brigade, which had reinforced Gregg, was finally dismounted, and assaulting through an opening near the centre of the line, the temporary works were carried by the entire Union line, and the position was won. Although the battle took place immediately in front of the Federal infantry, General Meade declined to put the latter into action, and the battle was won by the cavalry alone. The result gave possession of the cross-roads, and showed Grant that Lee's army was retiring by the right flank.

The night following the battle Sheridan withdrew the two cavalry divisions to the left rear of the army, and, marching to Old Church, threw out pickets towards Cold

2. After Stuart's death, the Confederate cavalry was reorganized in three divisions under Hampton, Fitzhugh Lee, and W. H. P. Lee, due to reinforcement by Butler's cavalry brigade from South Carolina.

Harbour, the possession of which was necessary to secure White House as a base. The enemy realized this too, and a fierce fight ensued at Matadequin Creek, in which the Confederate force was finally driven to Cold Harbour, that town being taken the following day (May 31st), after a hard-fought battle.

The cavalry at Cold Harbour was now so isolated, being nine miles from the nearest infantry, that Sheridan was making preparations to withdraw, when he received word from Meade to hold the town at all hazards. Its capture by the cavalry had not been anticipated by Grant.

Accordingly Sheridan made every preparation during the night to hold the town; and on the following day, behind his temporary breastworks, successfully met and repulsed the Confederate infantry under Kershaw. About 10 o'clock a. m. the cavalry was relieved by the Sixth Army Corps, and was moved to a position at Bottom's Bridge, on the north side of the Chickahominy, where it rested in camp until June 6th.

Wilson having meanwhile driven the enemy out of Hawes' Shop and passed so far around Lee's left flank as to deceive him into the belief that he was threatened by a large force, after taking a number of prisoners, fell back the next day and quietly went into camp at New Castle Ferry.

Grant's unsuccessful attack upon the enemy's strong position at Cold Harbour made him decide to again move his army forward by the left flank. To draw off the enemy's cavalry during this dangerous manoeuvre, Sheridan received instructions on June 6th to proceed with two cavalry divisions *via* Charlottesville to break up the Virginia Central Railroad, and afterwards to unite, if possible, with the army advancing through West Virginia under General Hunter towards Lynchburg.

Wilson's division was directed to remain with the Army

of the Potomac, receiving its instructions direct from army headquarters. Torbert's and Gregg's divisions accordingly started on the 7th of June, taking with them three days rations in haversacks to last for live days, two days forage on the pommels of saddles, and 100 rounds of ammunition to each man.

The line of march carried the command through New Castle and Polecat Station along the north bank of the North Anna, through Twyman's Store, and across the Anna on the 10th instant, and in the vicinity of Trevilian Station on the 11th.

Here Torbert's division, pressing back the enemy's pickets, found the enemy in force about three miles from Trevilian, posted behind heavy timber. At the same time, Custer was sent by a wood road to destroy Trevilian Station. In doing this Custer passed between Fitzhugh Lee's and Hampton's divisions, and soon had possession of the station, as well as the Confederate wagons, caissons, and led horses, causing Hampton to detach Rosser's brigade.

Assured of Custer's position, Sheridan dismounted Torbert's two remaining brigades, and, aided by one of Gregg's brigades carried the enemy's works, driving Hampton's division pell-mell back on Custer, and even through his lines. Gregg's remaining brigade had mean while attacked Fitzhugh Lee successfully, and pursued him until almost dark as far as Louisa Court House. Hampton's scattered forces retreated towards Gordonsville, and were joined by Fitzhugh Lee's command during the night.

The cavalry corps encamped that night at Trevilian, and here Sheridan received information which showed that General Hunter was marching away from, instead of towards, Charlottesville. He therefore decided to give up attempting to join Hunter, and made immediate preparations to return to the Army of the Potomac. The wounded and prisoners greatly impeded his movements, and his supply of ammunition was not sufficiently large for more than one general engagement.

On the morning of June 12th Gregg's division proceeded to destroy the railroad towards Louisa Court House, while Torbert made a reconnaissance towards Gordonsville. The latter became heavily engaged with Hampton's and Fitzhugh Lee's cavalry at Mallory's Cross-Roads, about two miles beyond Trevilian, the battle continuing until dark.

Although the fighting in this series of engagements was in favour of Sheridan, the general result prevented a return by way of Mallory's Ford, as had been planned, and Sheridan decided forthwith to return by the same road on which lit had come. But for reasons which are not clear he marched north-east, reaching Catharpen road, in the Wilderness, on the 14th; on the 15th, the Ta River; on the 16th, it passed through Bowling Green to the Mattapony River; on the 17th, it reached Walkerton, and on the 18th, the vicinity of King and Queen County. On the 19th instant the wounded, the prisoners, and about 2,000 contrabands were sent to White House, while the corps marched to Dunkirk, reaching White House on the 28th of June.

At the latter place Sheridan found orders directing him to break up the supply station there and conduct the 900 wagons to Petersburg. This was successfully accomplished, but not without several severe engagements with the Confederate cavalry, which had again got across his line of march. Gregg's division had a severe engagement at St. Mary's Church, particularly creditable to the cavalry.

In combination with the operations of the Army of the Potomac, the Army of the James, under General Butler, had meanwhile moved up the Peninsula; and on May 5th General Kautz, with a cavalry force of nearly 8,000 men,[3] had been detached for a raid against the Petersburg & Weldon Railroad. Kautz forced the Blackwater, burned the railroad bridge at Stony Creek below Petersburg, cut the Danville Railroad at three points, cut the Petersburg & Lynchburg Railroad at three points, cut the Petersburg & Weldon Railroad, and destroyed property of immense value. The command reached City Point in safety on May 17th, having marched from thirty to forty miles a day for six days. On June 9th General Kautz, with 1,300 cavalry, took active part in the movement which General Butler had planned for the capture of Petersburg, then defended by a force of about 1,200 militia. It was arranged that Kautz should make a detour to the left, attacking the city from the Jerusalem road, while the infantry forces under General Gillmore should cooperate on the Jordan's Point and City Point roads. Kautz's cavalry—a portion mounted and the remainder dismounted—gallantly charged the enemy's entrenchments, capturing the works and approaching very near the city, but, owing to lack of support from the infantry, the cavalry was obliged to fall back.[4]

Wilson's division, augmented to 5,500 men by the addition of the cavalry from the Army of the James, had, during the absence of the other divisions of the Cavalry Corps at Trevilian Station, made a raid (July 22nd) south of Petersburg, destroying the Petersburg & Lynchburg and Richmond & Danville railroads. Upon reaching the left of the army on his return, Wilson was attacked in front by a large force of Confederate infantry under General Mahone, sent down from Petersburg on the Weldon Rail-

---

3. First Brigade: Third New York Cavalry, First District of Columbia Cavalry. Second Brigade: Fifth Pennsylvania Cavalry, Eleventh Pennsylvania Cavalry, section of Eighth New York Artillery. Total, 2,838 men for duty, equipped.
4. General Gillmore's alleged bad management of this attacked to charges against him by General Butler, and his subsequent relief from command at his own request.

road, and on the flank by the Confederate cavalry, which had dropped Sheridan and marched rapidly to this point. The impossibility of breaking the infantry line which confronted it caused the division to fall back across the Nottoway and Meherrin rivers, and swing east across the Blackwater, losing in the retreat a great number of horses through heat and fatigue. Wilson had previously expressed his doubts of being able to return safely, unless the enemy's cavalry and infantry were kept engaged by General Sheridan and the Army of the Potomac respectively. But the destruction of the railroads on this raid was considered by General Grant to have more than compensated for the severe losses which the cavalry division sustained. Had infantry been promptly sent, as requested, to meet Wilson at Ream's Station, only four miles from Meade's headquarters, and open the door for his return, he could have safely with drawn his command and rejoined the army without material loss.

From the 2n to the 26th of July Sheridan was at Lighthouse Point recuperating his hard-worked command. Here 1,500 horses were received in addition to the 400 received at White House. That the Union cavalry had learned to take better care of its horse-flesh is shown from the fact that these 1,900 remounts were all that the Cavalry Corps received from the Quartermaster's Department of the Army while Sheridan had personal command that is, from April 6th to August 1st.

The misfortunes of the national cavalry during this period was due to its division into two parts, and although it had been roughly handled, it was soon ready for active operations. On the afternoon of July 26th the First and Second Cavalry Divisions moved north of the James, the Second Army Corps cooperating, with orders to raid, if opportunity offered, the Virginia Central Railroad, and destroy the bridges over the North and South Anna rivers. The Appomattox was crossed at Broadway Landing; and at Deep Bottom, Kautz's small cavalry division joined the raiding force, the Second Army Corps taking the advance.

A portion of Hancock's corps soon became engaged, and Sheridan with two divisions of the cavalry accordingly moved to the right upon the strongly fortified New Market and Central roads, leading to Richmond. In advance of Ruffin's House on the New Market road, the First and Second Cavalry Divisions formed line of battle, but were driven back over the high ground by the Confederate infantry divisions of Kershaw, Wilcox, and Heath. Reaching the eastern extremity of a ridge, the cavalry were quickly dismounted and directed to lie down about fifteen yards from the crest. When the enemy's infantry arrived, such a galling fire was delivered from the cavalry's repeating carbines that the Confederate divisions gave way in disorder. The Federal cavalry quickly followed, capturing 250 prisoners and two battle-flags. This adaptability to fight mounted or dismounted had now become a marked characteristic of the Union cavalry.

The long line presented by the cavalry and the Second Army Corps deceived General Lee into the belief that Grant had transferred a large part of his force to the north side of the James. Lee accordingly moved a large body of his troops from Petersburg to the vicinity of New Market. This was one of the very objects which Grant wished to obtain by this demonstration north of the James, as the explosion of the mine at Petersburg was nearing consummation, by means of which he hoped to gain possession of the city.

Giving up all idea then of the original objects of the expedition, Hancock and Sheridan bent all their resources towards keeping up the deception without giving battle.

This was accomplished until the 29th instant, when the Second Corps was withdrawn to take part in the assault on Petersburg the following day.

This withdrawal of the infantry left the cavalry corps in a position where it could have been annihilated had the enemy seen fit to attack. But shortly after daylight on the 30th the cavalry safely followed the infantry, and moved with a view to operating on the enemy's left flank, should the mine explosion be successful. The failure, however, of the latter caused this movement of the cavalry to be at once arrested. On August 1st, two days after the mine explosion, General Sheridan was relieved from personal command of the Cavalry Corps, and was ordered to the Shenandoah Valley.

The results thus far accomplished by the cavalry under Sheridan had been most distinguished. With the idea ever held in view that the Cavalry Corps should be organized and used to fight the enemy's cavalry, he had succeeded in almost annihilating what had heretofore been the most uniformly successful arm of the Confederate Army. Besides accomplishing the destruction of millions of dollars' worth of property, the Cavalry Corps had, in all important movements, acted as a screen to the main army, and by its hostile demonstrations had time after time forced the Confederate commander-in-chief, much against his will, to detach much-needed troops from his already hard-pressed army. Had it been kept united in its more important operations of breaking up the enemy's communications, it would have escaped all defeat and would have been much more successful.

CHAPTER 17

Kanawha & Shenandoah Valley

The Federal Government had, with an inconsiderable force, been able to hold the State of West Virginia, subject though it was at all times to guerrilla operations and to bold raids of the enemy's cavalry. Aside from the moral effect of keeping the State within the Union, the Baltimore & Ohio Railroad in the northern part, main line between the East and West, the Virginia Central Railroad, penetrating the Blue Ridge at Rockfish Gap, and the Virginia & Tennessee Railroad, just beyond West Virginia's southern boundary, were all of immense strategic importance.

But although the State had by extraordinary exertions been held, the operations of the cavalry had been inconspicuous. With the advent of Grant's control of the Federal armies, the cavalry of the Army of West Virginia came into more prominence.

In the spring of 1864 the Department of West Virginia, which included the Shenandoah Valley, was in command of General Sigel, who, under orders from Grant, despatched an expedition under General Crook to cut the Virginia & Tennessee Railroad at New River Bridge and destroy the salt works at Saltville. As a diversion, Sigel proposed to menace the Virginia Central Railroad at Staunton.

Crook entrusted the destruction of the works at Saltville to General Averell's cavalry division, while he himself marched against New River Bridge. It is with the cavalry command that we are chiefly interested.

Averell was at Charleston, W. Va., with 2,479 officers and men[1] when Crook's orders reached him. Marching on May 1st over pathless mountains, Averell found Saltville too strongly guarded to be taken without infantry and artillery. Approaching Wytheville on the 10th, he was confronted by 5,000 of the enemy under Generals Morgan and Jones, whom he successfully attacked and held at bay for the purpose of preventing their concentration on General Crook's column. Proceeding to New River, Averell crossed at an opportune time, the river rising in time to check Morgan's pursuing force. At Christianburg, Averell took two 3-inch guns and destroyed the railroad to a point four miles east of town. On the 15th instant the little command rejoined General Crook at Union, having marched with uncomplaining fortitude 350 miles through an almost impassable region, destitute of supplies, thirty miles of the journey being made in single file, on foot, over unfrequented paths.

While this campaign of the Kanawha was taking place, Sigel had, with 6,000 men, of which 1,000 were cavalry under General Stahel (an officer of foreign birth), begun operations in the Shenandoah Valley. He reports: "The few troops I have here [at Winchester] are excellent, with the exception of the cavalry."

On May 15th he met the Confederate force under Breckenridge, at New Market,[2] and the Federal cavalry, posted on the left of the lines, were routed early in the action.

---

1. Averell's brigade commanders were General Duffié and Colonel Schoonmaker.

2. Breckenridge had 5,500 men, his 800 cavalry being commanded by Imboden. The corps of cadets of the Virginia Military Institute, under Colonel Shipp, took part in this battle.

Although the remainder of the Union troops contested the ground bravely, they finally gave way. Sigel was signally defeated, and was accordingly relieved from command of the Department of West Virginia, being succeeded on May 21st by General Hunter.

On May 26th Hunter began from Cedar Creek the campaign which had for its object the occupation of Lynchburg. His two cavalry divisions were under the command of Duffié (also a foreigner) and Averell.

The Federal command encountered no opposition until it reached Harrisonburg, where Imboden was found occupying a strong position. The Federal cavalry succeeded in capturing a large supply train at this point. On the 5th of June, Wyncoop's cavalry brigade took an active and important part in the battle of Piedmont, by which the Confederate General Jones was defeated; on the 6th Hunter occupied Staunton, and on the 8th he was reinforced by the infantry under Crook and the cavalry under Averell.

In setting out from Staunton, Duffié's cavalry division was ordered to demonstrate against the enemy at Waynesborough, but finding the Confederate force very strong, he crossed the Blue Ridge and cut the Charlottesville & Lynchburg Railroad at Arlington Station. Imboden followed him, but was repulsed with loss, Duffié capturing 100 prisoners, including seventeen officers. While these operations were highly successful, Duffié's failure to return to the main command caused Hunter a long delay at Staunton, and the main objective, Lynchburg, was reinforced before the Federal troops arrived.

On the 17th Averell, supported by Duffié, came upon the enemy at Quaker Church, five miles from Lynchburg;, and, aided by Crook's infantry, charged their entrenchments and carried the works. But finding Lynchburg heavily reinforced, Hunter decided to withdraw toward his base by way of Buford's Pass. This he accomplished successfully, Early following, and repulsed the enemy whenever attacked. He reached Salem on the 21st instant, where the enemy abandoned the pursuit, and arrived, half-starved at Granley's Bridge on the 27th.

Hunter's campaign had the effect of drawing off a portion of Lee's force to reinforce Lynchburg, and caused a great loss of property to the Confederate Government. In these successes the cavalry divisions of Generals Averell and Duffié took a prominent part.

But Early did not long remain idle. After forcing Hunter into the Shenandoah a manoeuvre which freed Lynchburg and left the lower Shenandoah open he united General Breckenridge's infantry division and the cavalry of General Robert Ransom, Jr., to his own corps and moved down the valley. Reaching Winchester on July 2nd, and Martinsburg two days later, he brushed Sigel's and Wallace's troops aside, crossed the Potomac, and threatened Washington. This movement so alarmed the Federal authorities that the Sixth and Nineteenth Army Corps were rapidly transferred from the Army of the Potomac to Washington, resulting in Early's retiring through Leesburg, Winchester, and Strasburg. During this retreat Early was continually harassed by Duffié's cavalry division, which attacked his trains and engaged in several severe skirmishes.

On the 24th of July, Early turned at Kernstown on Crook's command, which was following him, and handled it so severely that Crook was obliged to retire to Harper's Ferry. In this battle both Duffié's and Averell's cavalry saw severe service, but that their efficiency was not what it should have been is shown by Hunter's letter to Halleck, written about this time: "The cavalry and the dismounted men in the late fights behaved in the most disgraceful manner, their officers in many instances leading them off and starting all kinds of lying reports tending to demoralize the whole command." Although applicable to the dismounted men, who were the odds and ends of various regiments about Washington, this statement was unjust to the main cavalry force, which, with few exceptions, fought gallantly,

The way was again open for Early, and, advancing into Maryland, he detached McCausland to Chambersburg, Penn., laid that town in ashes, and fell back towards Strasburg.

CHAPTER 18

Campaign of the Opequon

Early's second raid caused such consternation in the North that Grant determined to not only crush Early's command, but, by devastating the fertile valley of the Shenandoah, to prevent its being used in future as a base of supplies for the Confederate armies. General Sheridan was selected to carry out this difficult task, in a region where many generals had already failed.

When Sheridan assumed command of the Army of the Shenandoah, its strength comprised the Sixth Army Corps, one division of the Nineteenth Army Corps, two divisions of infantry from West Virginia, and Torbert's division of cavalry. In the expectation that Averell's cavalry division would soon join him, Sheridan appointed Torbert chief-of-cavalry, and as signed Merritt to the command of Torbert's old division.

Sheridan's instructions directed him to mass his troops at Harper's Ferry, and follow and attack the raiding force wherever found. And, although protecting all buildings, to take and destroy all forage and stock in the valley which might invite the enemy's return. The first five weeks of Sheridan's Valley campaign were spent in manoeuvrings, offensive and defensive, which, though enlivened by numerous severe cavalry skirmishes, brought on no general action.

The Federal Army set out from Harper's Ferry on August 10th, and between that date and the 13th moved with strategical precision to Strasburg. Here Sheridan received a delayed letter from Grant to Halleck, informing him that Early had been reinforced by infantry and artillery from the Confederate Army at Petersburg, and directing Sheridan to act on the defensive. The latter accordingly retraced his forward movement with the same precision which had marked his advance, and left in his wake a devastated valley. By August 18th he was again in the vicinity of Charlestown, closely followed by Early; but towards the end of the month the Confederate general fell back towards Brucetown and Bunker Hill, and later to the vicinity of Stephenson's Depôt, near Winchester. No engagement of importance occurred,[1] Sheridan standing strictly on the defensive, as his orders required, in spite of great political pressure employed to force him into aggressive action. But the time was well employed. As Sheridan reports: "The cavalry was employed every day in harassing the enemy, its opponents being principally infantry. In these skirmishes the cavalry was becoming educated to attack infantry lines."

September 16th Sheridan learned through spies that Kershaw's division had returned to the Army of Northern Virginia, and he decided that the time for active operations had at length come.

His original plan of action contemplated throwing his army across the Valley Pike at Newtown, south of Winchester, but hearing from Averell that on the 17th Early had attacked him at Bunker Hill with two infantry divisions, and had afterwards proceeded to wards Martinsburg, he determined to attack the two remaining Confederate

---

1. On September 13th McIntosh's brigade of Wilson's division (Second Ohio, Third New Jersey, Fifth New York, Second New York, and First Connecticut) captured the Eighth South Carolina Infantry, with its colonel and battle-flag, at Abraham's Creek.

divisions at Stephenson's Depot, and then turn, in time to meet those at Bunker Hill and Martinsburg.

But Early, suspecting that Sheridan was about to move, promptly withdrew these divisions, so that on the 18th instant Gordon's division was at Bunker Hill, Ramseur's two miles east of Winchester across the Berryville Pike, Wharton's at Stephenson's, and Rode's division near there. The cavalry of Lomax, Jackson, and Johnson was to the right of Ramseur, while Fitzhugh Lee covered Stephenson's Depôt, westward.

On September 19th Sheridan's army was up and moving at 3 o'clock in the morning. Wilson's division crossed the Opequon at the Berryville crossing, and, charging up the canon through which the Berryville- Winchester turnpike runs, captured a small work on the open ground at its mouth before the Confederates could recover from their astonishment. All efforts to dislodge Wilson proved fruitless, and he held it until the arrival of the Sixth Army Corps. This corps and the Nineteenth, which were following Wilson, were so long passing the defile already referred to, that it was late in the forenoon before they were able to form line of battle; and in the meanwhile Early had time to bring Bodes and Gordon's infantry divisions down from Stephenson's, and from the high ground in front was able to enfilade the Union troops as they advanced. With the arrival of the infantry, Wilson moved to the left from his perilous position in front and took position along the south bank of Abraham's Creek, covering the Union left.

Line of battle formed, the Union infantry advanced Getty's division of the Sixth Corps to the left, and Rickett's division to the right of the Berryville-Winchester pike; Grover's division of the Nineteenth Corps to the right of Rickett's, with Russell's and Dwight's divisions in reserve, in rear of their respective corps. The advance was successfully accomplished on the left, but retarded on the right;

and as Getty and Rickett gained ground to the left, a serious break occurred at the centre of the line, which was opportunely filled by Russell's reserve division.

Meanwhile Averell had advanced from Darksville southward; Custer had crossed the Opequon at Lock's Ford, while Lowell and Devin had crossed at Ridgway's Ford, all three commands pressing forward towards Stephenson's Depôt. To confront this force, the Confederates had Patton's brigade of infantry and some of Fitzhugh Lee's cavalry, but with Averell's division on the west of the Valley Pike, and Merritt's on the east, Torbert easily drove this force towards Winchester. The ground in front of the Federal cavalry was well adapted for a charge, and while Averell pressed rapidly towards the Confederate rear, Merritt's division charged forward with such success as to break the Confederate left and capture a battery of five guns and 1,200 prisoners.

Almost simultaneous with this, Crook's divisions, which had been massed at the Berryville crossing of the Opequon, were hurled against the Confederate left, on the right of the Nineteenth Army Corps. This, together with the brilliant success of Torbert's cavalry along the Valley Pike, stampeded the whole Confederate line, which fell back in confusion towards Winchester in spite of the repeated efforts of its commanders to rally their demoralized units.

Sheridan had hoped to retain Crook's divisions in reserve, until an opportunity should occur to use them in taking possession of the Valley Pike, southward, thus cutting off the enemy's retreat. But under the circumstances it had seemed best to place Crook's command in the main line of battle to the right. Accordingly, Wilson was directed to perform alone, as well as he was able, what had been intended for Crook's entire command to prevent the retreat of the Confederate army along the Valley Pike towards Strasburg.

Wilson's demonstrations on the extreme Confederate right had, earlier in the battle, caused Early to weaken Fitzhugh Lee's cavalry division on the left by detaching Wickham's brigade for the purpose of securing a route for retreat; but this brigade was later sent back to the Confederate left to confront Averell, so that Wilson advanced without difficulty, scattering Wickham's brigade and continuing his advance till after night.

When the Confederate line fell back panic-stricken, Sheridan caused the Sixth and Nineteenth Army Corps to move towards the left to assist Wilson in taking possession of the Valley Pike. But Ramseur's Confederate division, which still retained its morale, was in position to delay movements in this direction till the Confederates had swept by the point of danger and darkness had put an end to hostile operations.

The Union loss in this battle of the Opequon was from 4,500 to 5,000 men, of which the cavalry lost but 441. The Confederate loss amounted to about 4,000, of which nearly 2,000 were prisoners. The Army of the Shenandoah also captured five pieces of artillery and nine battle-flags.

The victory came at a time when its moral effect was most needed, and crowned with success a long series of misfortunes to the Federal arms in the Shenandoah Valley. It restored the lower valley to Federal control, and relieved Maryland, Pennsylvania, and the national capital from further fears of invasion, and it is safe to say could not have been gained but for the part taken by the cavalry both in securing and driving the enemy from it.

CHAPTER 19

Milford to Tom's Brook

"We have just sent them whirling through Winchester, and we are after them tomorrow," wired Sheridan, and his words sent a thrill of joy through the Northern States.

In obedience to Sheridan's orders, the cavalry corps was after the retreating Confederates at daybreak, September 20th Merritt straight down the Valley Road towards Strasburg; Wilson to Front Royal by way of Stevensburg; and Averell along the Back Bond, skirting the edge of the mountain range to the west, towards Cedar Creek. The infantry followed, the Nineteenth Corps on the right of the pike, the Sixth on the left, and the Eighth Corps in the rear. Early had taken his stand at Fisher's Hill, two miles south of Strasburg and beyond a little stream called Tumbling Run. No effort was for the present made to dislodge him, for his position was probably the strongest that he could have selected.

At Strasburg the valley is divided longitudinally by the Massanutton Range, and between this range and the Little North Mountains to the west is barely four miles. With his right resting on the Massanutton spurs and the north fork of the Shenandoah, his infantry line of battle extended across the valley, and was prolonged on the left by Lomax's cavalry, dismounted. The whole Confederate line was entrenched, and so sure was Early of the strength of his position that the ammunition chests were lifted from the caissons and placed behind the works.

As the Union troops arrived on the evening of the 20th, Wright and Emory went into position on the heights of Strasburg, Crook north of Cedar Creek, and the cavalry to the right and rear of Wright and Emory, extending to the Back Road.

A reconnaissance satisfied Sheridan that the enemy's right was impregnable, and he determined to use the same turning tactics he had used at Opequon.

On the 21st Sheridan pushed the enemy's skirmishers back towards Fisher's Hill, and after a severe engagement of the infantry, secured an advantageous position on the right. The night of the 21st Crook was concealed in the timber near Strasburg. The same day Torbert, with Wilson's and Merritt's cavalry divisions, was dispatched up the Luray Valley with orders to defeat the enemy's cavalry, cross over the Massanutton Range to New Market, and thus gain the enemy's rear, should Sheridan drive him south from Fisher's Hill.

On the 22nd Crook moved secretly to a position in the timber near Little North Mountain, and the Sixth and Nineteenth Corps were massed opposite the right centre of the enemy's line, Rickett's division opposite the left centre, and Averell's cavalry on Rickett's right.

The manoeuvre of Crook was eminently successful. Moving out from the timber late in the afternoon of September 22nd, he struck the enemy's left and rear with unexpected and irresistible force; the infantry in the main line of battle swung into the turning movement at the proper time, and the rout of Early's army was complete.

All during the night of the 22nd the Federal infantry with Devin's brigade of cavalry pushed on in pursuit of the demoralized enemy. Devin struck the enemy north of Mount Jackson, and had he been properly supported by Averell, would doubtless have taken thousands of prisoners. But for some unaccountable reason Averell had gone into camp immediately after the battle of Fisher's Hill, leaving the infantry and Devin's small cavalry brigade to make the all-night pursuit. He reinforced Devin about 3 p. m. on the 23rd at Mount Jackson, but his attack was indifferently made, and he soon afterwards withdrew into camp near Hawkinsburg.

Meanwhile Torbert with his cavalry had passed up the Luray Valley to Milford, and finding this place in possession of the Confederate cavalry under Wickham, the bridges destroyed and the country impracticable for cavalry off the turnpike, it was impossible to dislodge the enemy or to pass beyond the defile opposite New Market. "Not knowing these facts, I was astonished and chagrined," writes Sheridan, "on the morning of the 23rd at Woodstock, to receive the intelligence that he [Torbert] had fallen back to Front Royal and Buckton Ford."

Had Torbert succeeded in forcing the pass and reaching New Market, as Sheridan contemplated, Early's army must have been captured bodily. As it was, Sheridan's loss was only about 400, while Early's was between 1,300 and 1,400. Early abandoned most of his artillery, and such property as was within his field works.

Excepting Devin's energetic pursuit, it must be confessed that the cavalry contributed very little to the success of the battle of Fisher's Hill; but candour compels the statement that the valleys were too narrow for cavalry operations. Averell was immediately relieved from his command, Sheridan attributing his apparent apathy to dissatisfaction at Torbert's appointment as chief-of-cavalry, which had repeatedly manifested itself, except when Averell was conducting independent expeditions. Colonel William H. Powell succeeded to the command of Averell's division. The enemy which had concentrated south of Mount Jackson was driven thirteen miles southward on the 24th, through New Market and Keezletown, reaching Port Republic during the night, and moving from thence to Brown's Gap in the Blue Ridge. Below Port Republic, Early had been joined by Lomax's, Wickham's, and Payne's brigades of cavalry, and Kershaw's infantry division, while Cutshaw's artillery was *en route* to join him.

On the 25th the Sixth and Nineteenth Army Corps reached Harrisonburg, where they were ordered for the present to remain; and during the next few days the cavalry, all of which had rejoined Sheridan by the 26th, was employed in laying waste the upper valley, and in skirmishing with the enemy as far south as Staunton and Brown's Gap, the general line of the Federal army being until October 6th from Port Republic along North River by Mount Crawford to the Back Road near the mouth of Briery Branch Gap.

During this time Sheridan advised that the Valley campaign be here terminated, and that a portion, at least, of the troops be withdrawn for other purposes. Grant's consent to Sheridan's plans reached the latter October 5th, and on the following day the movement down the valley was begun, the infantry preceding the cavalry, and the latter in a line stretching completely across the valley, destroying or taking all available supplies.

The enemy's cavalry, now under General Rosser,[1] became exceedingly annoying to the rear guard during the next few days, and, on October 8th, Torbert was directed by Sheridan "to give Rosser a drubbing next morning or get whipped himself." At this time Merritt was in camp near

1. Rosser had joined Early on October 5th, with a cavalry brigade from Richmond, and was boastfully proclaimed "the saviour of the valley."

Round Top, north of Tom's Brook, and Custer some six miles north-west, near Tumbling Run.

During the night Custer was ordered to retrace his steps by the back road, joining his line of battle with Merritt, who was to attack along the Valley Pike, only about three miles separating these parallel roads.

About 7 a. m. October 9th Custer encountered Rosser with three brigades near Tom's Brook Crossing, and soon after Merritt struck Lomax and Johnson on the Valley Pike, the Federal line of battle extending across the valley.

The fighting was desperate on both sides. On the Federal side there was a determination to maintain the prestige of the cavalry in the valley, and to make up for Torbert's failure to punish these same Confederate divisions at Milford a few weeks before. On the Confederate side it was hoped that Rosser, whose previous efforts had been successful, would re-establish the supremacy of the Confederate cavalry, and the sight of the devastated valley by men, many of whom were from this region, spurred them to stubborn resistance.

The fight was essentially a sabre contest. Again and again were charges given and received on both sides, and for two hours the honours were almost equally divided, the Confederates holding the centre with success, while the Federal cavalry pushed back the flanks. This finally proved too much for the enemy, and as both Confederate flanks gave way, Merritt and Custer ordered a charge along the whole line. The retreat of the Confederates which immediately followed degenerated into a panic-stricken rout, which continued for twenty-six miles up the valley, through Mount Jackson and Columbia Furnaces. Eleven pieces of artillery, 330 prisoners, ambulances, caissons, and even the headquarters wagons of the Confederate commanders, were captured.

Torbert has stated that of all the cavalry victories, that of

Tom's Brook "was the most brilliant one of them all, and the most decisive the country has ever witnessed."

Of this reverse to the Confederate arms Early wrote to Lee, October 9th; "God knows I have done all in my power to avert the disasters which have befallen the command; but the fact is, the enemy's cavalry is so much superior to ours, both in numbers and equipment, and the country is so favour able to the operations of cavalry that it is impossible for ours to compete with his. Lomax's cavalry are armed entirely with rifles, and have no sabres, and the consequence is that they cannot fight on horse back, and in the open country they cannot successfully fight on foot against large bodies of cavalry. It would be better if they could all be put in the infantry; but if that were tried, I am afraid they would all run off."[2]

Sheridan had specially halted the Union infantry one day in order to have the battle of Tom's Brook fought. On the following day he again moved forward across Cedar Creek and occupied the heights, the cavalry on the flanks, and the Sixth Corps continuing its march to Front Royal, with a view of joining the Army of the Potomac. On the 13th, however, it was recalled in consequence of the enemy's arrival at Fisher's Hill. It was Sheridan's intention at the time to send all the cavalry on a raid through Chester Gap to the Virginia Central Railroad at Charlottesville, and it had actually proceeded as far as Front Royal, but in consequence of unconfirmed information that Longstreet was about to join Early, the expedition was given up. The cavalry was accordingly ordered back to Cedar Creek, and General Wright was directed to make his position strong, and be well prepared for any advance of the enemy. This done, Sheridan proceeded to Washington to consult with the Secretary of War in regard to future operations.

---

2. *Rebellion Records*, page 558, Vol. 43, Part 1.

CHAPTER 20

Cedar Creek to Liberty Mills

Nothing suspicious was seen or heard by the Federal army at Cedar Creek to indicate a further advance by Early. In fact, a reconnaissance on October 18th reported the enemy as having retreated up the valley. But it is to be observed that no cavalry scouts or pickets were kept in advance to observe the enemy's movements.

On the night of the 18th the Army of the Shenandoah was encamped on the bluffs along the north bank of Cedar Creek, as follows: Crook's Army of West Virginia was on the extreme left, his two divisions on each side of the pike; on his right was the Nineteenth Corps, separated from the Sixth Corps farther to the right by a rivulet Meadow Brook; Merritt's cavalry division was on the right of the Sixth Corps at Middle Marsh Brook, and Custer's a mile and a half beyond Merritt, watching the fords of the Back and Mine Bank roads; Powell's First Brigade was out on the Front Royal pike, and his Second Brigade was guarding Burton's Ford on the Shenandoah.

The enemy attacked the left of the line, in a heavy fog before daylight, October 19th, and, with a turning movement which was very effective, drove the infantry back from position to position.

The cavalry was in the saddle at the first alarm, and

was put in position on the right of the infantry. The First Brigade, Second Division, being at Burton's Ford, was cut off by the enemy's attack, but, passing completely about the Confederate flank, joined the left of the army at Middletown. The second brigade of this division moved slowly backward on the Front Royal Winchester pike, and succeeded admirably in engaging Lomax's cavalry and in preventing him, throughout the day, from attacking the Federal rear. The value of this stubborn resistance can best be estimated by thinking of the consternation that would have followed an attack on the rear, in addition to the confusion in front.

Of Merritt's division, the Reserve Brigade, having received orders for a reconnaissance the night before, had already advanced to the line of pickets, when the latter were attacked, but subsequently fell back, and gave way to the First Brigade. Custer's division, which had at daylight been feebly attacked by Rosser at Copp's Ford, was, with Merritt's division, deployed in line of battle on the right of the infantry. The infantry lines soon after gave way in confusion, and the Fifth U. S. Cavalry was deployed across the fields in the almost useless attempt to stop stragglers and form a line. Devin's brigade was sent to the left of the line, with orders to hold the pike, and about 10 o'clock the First and Third Divisions[1] were transferred to the left of the line, across the pike just north of Middletown, the First Division being so disposed as to connect with the line of the infantry. The First Brigade, Second Division, was on the left of the Third Division, and the Third Division was on the left of the First.

The cavalry fought gallantly. Even at times when, by

---

1. Three regiments of the Third Division were left on the right of the line, and for five hours gallantly stemmed the tide of thousands of stragglers who were moving to the rear.

backward movements of the infantry line on the right, the First Cavalry Division was subjected to a galling cross-fire, the division stood firm, and both divisions suffered greatly from a murderous artillery fire.

But for the services of the cavalry at this time on the left flank, the enemy must surely have penetrated to the rear of the Federal army. The cavalry not only held its own on the left, but at one time so threatened to envelop Early's right that he was forced to crowd his troops farther east.

Finding his efforts of little avail against the solid front presented by the Sixth Army Corps and the cavalry. Early determined to try to force the Union flank. But, to his surprise and consternation, he found his own troops in no condition for such an attack. Early himself states: "So many of our men had stopped in the camp to plunder (in which I am sorry to say that officers participated), the country was so open, and the enemy's cavalry so strong, that I did not deem it prudent to press further, especially as Lomax had not come up."[2]

Affairs were at this stage when Sheridan, having made his historic ride, arrived on the field. He says: "On arriving at the front I found Merritt's and Custer's divisions of cavalry under Torbert, and General Getty's division of the Sixth Corps, opposing the enemy."

Custer's division was at once (11 a.m.) ordered to the right, and in a charge drove back the enemy's cavalry for a mile behind their infantry supports. The Nineteenth Corps and two remaining divisions of the Sixth Corps were also ordered to the front, and Sheridan personally supervised the formation of the line of battle in prolongation of Getty's line.

At 4 p.m. a general advance of the Federal lines was ordered, and as the enemy's line overlapped a portion of the Union right, McMillan's brigade cut off the Confederate

2. Early to Lee, the day after the battle.

flanking force. This done, Custer's division was ordered to charge. Leaving but three regiments to hold the Confederate cavalry in his front, Custer moved to the left, dividing the enemy's cavalry from his infantry, and charging across an open plain on the enemy's exposed flank. The effect was apparent before the charge was completed, thousands of the enemy throwing away their arms and crowding across Cedar Creek, a demoralized mob.

Meanwhile Merritt's division, on the extreme right of the line, had also gallantly moved forward in the general advance of the line. "The Reserve and Second Brigades charged into a living wall of the enemy, which, receiving the shock, emitted a leaden sheet of fire upon their devoted ranks"; while the First Brigade, in column of regiments in line, overwhelmed a battery and its supports, amid a perfect tempest of fire at close range. In this charge the fearless and chivalric Lowell received a mortal wound.

The cavalry on both flanks continued the pursuit across Cedar Creek, and even after dark charged and broke the last line the disorganized Confederates attempted to form. Darkness alone saved the greater part of Early's army from capture.

The cavalry alone captured forty-five pieces of artillery, thirty-two caissons, forty-six army wagons, 672 prisoners more than half the total number captured and a great deal of other property.

The services of the cavalry during the entire day were most distinguished and valuable, and in decided contrast to those of the Confederate cavalry. Neither Rosser nor Lomax, although striking for the Union lines at a time when the Federal infantry was most demoralized, were able to reach the pike; the former being easily repulsed by Custer, and the latter held at bay during the entire day by Powell. The fact that two of the cavalry divisions were about to depart upon a raid to the Virginia Central Railroad, and that their orders were countermanded at the last moment by Sheridan at Front Royal, shows how the smallest happenings may affect the fate of the greatest battles.[3]

Early's disorganized army reassembled at New Market, while Sheridan proceeded to Kernstown. From Stephenson's Depot to Harper's Ferry the railroad was reconstructed and arrangements made to detach troops to General Grant. On the night of November 11th General Early made a reconnaissance north of Cedar Creek, but hastily retired on the night of the following day, before troops could be sent against him. His cavalry, however, were not so fortunate. On the day following this reconnaissance General Powell's cavalry division attacked Lomax's cavalry at Nineveh, routing them, pursuing them two miles south of Front Royal, and capturing all their artillery (two guns), their ordnance train, and 180 prisoners. On the same day General Custer, moving on the Middle and Back roads, engaged Rosser's cavalry division north of Cedar Creek, routing it, driving it across Cedar Creek and capturing sixteen prisoners. The enemy's infantry was also successfully engaged on the Valley Pike by a portion of the First Cavalry Division under General Merritt.

Late in November (November 28th to December 3rd), General Merritt was sent with two brigades on an expedition into the Luray Valley for the purpose of operating against Mosby, and of rendering the valley useless as a base of supplies for the guerrillas in the future.

The division passed through Ashby's Gap of the Blue Ridge, and raiding columns were then detached which dev-

---

3. During the Shenandoah campaign the cavalry alone captured 2,556 prisoners, 71 guns, 29 battle-flags, 52 caissons, 105 army wagons, 2,557 horses, 1,000 horse equipments, and 7,152 beef cattle. It destroyed, among other things, 420,742 bushels of wheat, 780 barns, and 700,000 rounds of ammunition.

astated the country on each side of the general line of march. The guerrillas kept safely at a distance and avoided capture, but the destruction of property was enormous that destroyed by the Reserve Brigade alone aggregating $411,620.

In spite of the bitter cold weather, the cavalry was kept moving during December. On the 19th Torbert, with Merritt's and Powell's divisions, marched through Chester Gap for the purpose of striking the Virginia Central Railroad at Gordonsville, while Custer, as a diversion, proceeded up the valley. Torbert drove Jackson's cavalry division out of Madison Court House, and the latter formed a junction with McCauseland's division at Liberty Mills; but the combined force, General Lomax commanding, was signally defeated by Torbert and driven across the Rapidan. The bridge had been mined, and was blown up while the Federal cavalry were crossing in pursuit; but, by crossing by fords above and below, Torbert captured two pieces of artillery. He then proceeded towards Gordonsville, but found the enemy's infantry in such force that he returned. Custer had meanwhile been surprised in his camp at Lacy's Springs, both Rosser's and Payne's forces attacking him at daylight, and he was obliged to retire.

The weather was so intensely cold during these operations that horses and men suffered severely, and many men were badly frost-bitten. The expeditions practically closed the operations of the winter, and Sheridan's troops went into cantonment near Winchester. The Sixth Corps had been sent to Petersburg early in December, one division of Crook's corps to West Virginia, and the remainder to City Point, leaving Sheridan with but one division of the Nineteenth Army Corps and the cavalry.

CHAPTER 21

White's Tavern, Waynesboro & White House

While these stirring events had been taking place in the Shenandoah Valley, Gregg's cavalry division (still known as the Second Cavalry Division), on duty with the Army of the Potomac, had not been idle. Indeed, in consequence of the withdrawal of the other cavalry divisions to the Shenandoah Valley, it had rather more than its share of cavalry duty to perform.

When Kershaw's division of Lee's army was withdrawn to reinforce Early, the Second Cavalry Division, with the Second Army Corps (Hancock's), crossed the James at Deep Bottom, August 14th. On the 16th the Federal cavalry met the enemy's cavalry on the Charles City road, and drove them as far as White's Tavern. In these engagements Generals Chambliss and Girardey, of the Confederate army, were killed.

During the destruction of the Weldon Railroad which followed, the cavalry was on picket duty, but a portion of it, dismounted, took active part in the engagement at Ream's Station on August 25th, which resulted in the breaking of Hancock's line and the capture of five pieces of his artillery.[1]

---

1. For the organization of the cavalry, see Appendix 13.

No movements of consequence, except reconnaissances, now occurred until September 30th, when a demonstration was ordered on the left of the line, to prevent the enemy detaching troops to the north side of the James. In this movement two divisions of the Fifth Army Corps under General Warren, and two of the Ninth Army Corps under General Parke, moved from the left towards Poplar Spring Church and Peeble's Farm; the cavalry division at the same time moved to the left and rear. On October 1st Gregg was attacked by a large force of the enemy on the Duncan road, where he was guarding the rear and left of the movement, but he repulsed the attack with great loss, General Dunovant being among the Confederates killed. For some weeks the troops were employed in holding and fortifying the position thus gained.

On October 27th the cavalry division was placed under the orders of General Hancock, and, together with part of the Ninth, Fifth, and Second Corps, moved towards the left in reconnaissance. The Second Corps and the cavalry crossed Hatcher's Run on the Vaughan road, with slight opposition from the enemy's cavalry. On arriving at Gravelly Run, the enemy was found posted on the west side in a position of great natural strength. The First Maine and Sixth Ohio were dismounted, and, assisted by the Twenty-first Pennsylvania, mounted, drove the enemy's line back beyond the heights, the enemy breaking in confusion at the advance of the Second Corps. In the subsequent operations on the Boydton Plank Road, the cavalry was on the left of the Second Army Corps, and, with almost the entire division dismounted, repeatedly held the line against superior numbers of the enemy until he retired. On October 28th the troops were again withdrawn to the lines of entrenchments.

During November the division was employed on picket

and reconnaissance; and on December 7th, numbering 4,200 effective men, it was sent, under General Warren, with three divisions of the Fifth Corps, Mott's division of the Second Corps, and four batteries of artillery, to destroy the Weldon Railroad and interrupt the enemy's communications.

As the command reached the vicinity of the railroad General Gregg detached a force to destroy the railroad bridge over the Nottoway, and the cavalry continued the partial destruction of the railroad as far as Jarratt's Station. On December 9th the work of destruction continued, the cavalry clearing the enemy out of the way southward, and picketing the country north and east. At Three Creeks the Confederates had posted on the south bank two small field-guns and two hundred cavalry, the bridges having been destroyed and the fords obstructed; but dismounted men crossed and drove the enemy away. The railroad was destroyed for seventeen or eighteen miles, when, the command's supplies not justifying further operations, it returned to camp on December 12th.

Early in February the Second Cavalry Division proceeded *via* Beam's Station to Dinwiddie Court House without finding the enemy in any considerable force. On the following day, however, the division formed a junction with General Warren at Gravelly Run, and covered his movements to Hatcher's Run, the enemy following. With the First and Third Brigades dismounted and the Second Brigade mounted, the enemy was driven across the run, and the command bivouacked on the field of battle.

On February 9th General David McM. Gregg, who had for so long a time been so prominently and illustriously identified with the cavalry of the Army of the Potomac, was relieved from command, through the acceptance of his resignation, and General John I. Gregg assumed temporary command. General Davies, returning from leave later in the month, assumed command, and on March 27th he in turn was relieved by General Crook, who retained permanent command of the division.[2] During this period little of importance occurred, the division reporting on the 27th to General Sheridan for duty with the First and Third Cavalry Divisions, which had again joined the Army of the Potomac.[3]

The latter divisions had meanwhile, on February 27th, entered upon the final campaign, which was to clear the valley, once for all, of organized Confederate troops.

General Merritt, who had performed such distinguished services as a division commander, succeeded General Torbert as chief-of-cavalry. Torbert had disappointed Sheridan during the battle of Fisher's Hill and in the later expedition to Gordonsville. He seemed to lack self-reliance at critical times, and one of Sheridan's traits of character was that he took no chances. Sheridan's original plans, as directed by Grant, contemplated the destruction of the Virginia Central Railroad, the capture of Lynchburg if practicable, and a junction with Sherman's victorious army in North Carolina.

A small force of Rosser's cavalry was encountered March 1st at Mount Crawford, but was easily driven to Kline's Mills. At this time Early was at Staunton, but as Sheridan's command approached that place he retired to Waynesboro, where he occupied a line of breastworks along a ridge west of the town. Custer was dispatched towards Waynesboro, closely followed by Devin, and finding the Confederate left somewhat exposed, he sent dismounted regiments around this flank, while he, with two brigades, part mounted and part dismounted, assaulted in front.

---

2. Wilson meanwhile having been ordered west to reorganize and command Sherman's cavalry.

3. For the effective force of the First and Third Divisions February 28th, see Appendix 14.

The flanking movement was successful, and enabled Custer's line of battle to carry the breastworks. The Eighth New York and First Connecticut charged in column through the enemy's line, and the town of Waynesboro, and held the east bank of the South River, thus cutting off the enemy's line of retreat. All the Confederates surrendered except Rosser's command and a few general officers, the cavalry capturing seventeen battle-flags, 1,600 prisoners, and eleven pieces of artillery.

Continuing the march, Custer's division reached Charlottesville on the 3rd instant, but the muddy roads delayed the wagon train until the 5th. On the 8th Custer destroyed the railroad as far as Amherst Court House, sixteen miles from Lynchburg, while Devin, who had proceeded along the James, destroyed the canal.

The Confederates had meanwhile destroyed the bridges over the James, and, the river being so swollen as to be unfordable, Sheridan deemed a junction with Sherman impracticable. He therefore decided to still further destroy the Virginia Central Railroad and James River Canal, and then join the Army of the Potomac in front of Petersburg.

Columbia was reached on the 10th of March, where a halt of a day was made to allow the trains to catch up. From this point Merritt, with Custer's division, proceeded to Louisa Court House, destroying the Virginia Central as far as Frederick's Hall, while Custer destroyed it from the latter place to Beaver Dam Station.

Receiving word that Pickett's Confederate division with Fitzhugh Lee's cavalry were moving east from Lynchburg, and that Longstreet was assembling a force at Richmond to cut off Sheridan's junction with Grant, the raiding force now pushed on to Ashland; Merritt having marched from Frederick's Hall through Hanover Court House, and Custer crossing the South Anna on the Ground Squirrel Bridge.

The command reached White House *via* King William Court House on March 18th, where supplies were found, which Sheridan had requested to have ready.

The expedition had caused an immense amount of damage to the Confederate cause, with but slight loss to Sheridan's command. But, owing to the incessant rains, which lasted for sixteen days and nights, the almost impassable roads and the high water in the streams, the march was one of the greatest hardship.

At White House the command rested for five days and shod the horses. But the march from Winchester had been so severe upon the latter that there was not a sufficient number of remounts at White House to replace those disabled, so that the dismounted men were sent into camp near City Point.[4]

---

4. For abstract of returns of the cavalry for March, 1865, see Appendix 15.

CHAPTER 22

Petersburg to the 'Grand Review'

On March 24th General Sheridan moved from White House, crossed the James River at Jones Landing, and joined the Army of the Potomac in front of Petersburg on the 27th instant. But his force was still regarded as a separate army, and he received his orders direct from General Grant.

The effective force of the three divisions of cavalry aggregated 9,000 men.[1] Sheridan's general instructions from Grant were to move near or through Dinwiddie, reaching the right and rear of the Confederate army as soon as possible, but with no intention of attacking the enemy in his entrenched position. Should he remain entrenched, Sheridan was to cut loose and destroy the Danville and South Side railroads the only avenues of supply to Lee's army, and then either return to the Army of the Potomac, or join Sherman's army in North Carolina.

The general movement against the Confederate army began March 29th. The evening of that day the cavalry had reached Dinwiddie Court House, on the extreme left of the line, the nearest extremity of the infantry line being near the intersection of the Quaker Road with the Boydton Plank Road. The First and Second Divisions went into camp, covering the Vaughan, Flatfoot, Boydton Plank, and

---

1. For organization, March 29th to April 9th, see Appendix 16.

Five Fork roads, all intersecting at Dinwiddie, Custer's division remaining at Malone's Crossing to guard the trains.

The next day Devin's division was sent by General Merritt to get possession of Five Forks, Davies brigade of Crook's division in support. The reconnaissance showed the enemy to be in force at Five Forks on the White Oak road, and there was severe skirmishing. On the following day, March 31st, Merritt, with the First Division and Davies brigade of the Third Division, again advanced on Five Forks, while Crook, with his two other brigades, moved to the left and encountered the enemy at Chamberlain's Creek. But in the meantime Warren's army corps, which was next on the right of the cavalry, was driven back, leaving the cavalry at Five Forks to bear the brunt of the attack. In the very obstinate battle which ensued, the enemy was unable, with two divisions of infantry and all his cavalry, to push back the five cavalry brigades, which were dismounted on the open plain in front of Dinwiddie. The fighting continued until after dark, and the opposing lines of bivouac that night were not separated by more than a hundred yards.

Of this day's battle General Grant says: "Here Sheridan displayed great generalship. Instead of retreating with his whole command on the main army, to tell the story of superior forces encountered, he deployed his cavalry on foot, leaving only mounted men enough to take charge of the horses. This compelled the enemy to deploy over a vast extent of wooded and broken country, and made his progress slow."

On the morning of the 1st of April, Sheridan, reinforced by the Fifth Corps, and later by Mackenzie's cavalry division[2] (1,000 effective men) from the Army of the James, advanced again against Five Forks.

---

2. On March 20th General Kautz was relieved from command of this cavalry division and was succeeded by General R. S. Mackenzie, a young officer of engineers, not long out of West Point.

His plan of attack was to make a feint with the cavalry, to turn the enemy's right, but meantime bringing up the entire Fifth Corps to strike the enemy's left flank and crush the whole force if possible. The movement was hastened by the fact that two divisions of the Fifth Corps were at the time in rear of the enemy. The enemy's infantry had, in the hot pursuit of Sheridan to Dinwiddie, isolated itself, and was, moreover, outside the Confederate line of works.

Warren's corps was slow getting up, but nevertheless Devin's and Custer's divisions were all the morning, under Merritt's direction, pressing the enemy steadily backward, until at 2 o'clock the Confederates were driven behind the works on the White Oak road.

In furtherance of the plan of attack Merritt closely engaged the enemy, and Warren's corps was ordered up on the Gravelly Church road, oblique to the White Oak road, and about one mile from Five Forks. But Warren was again slow in getting into position.

About 4 o'clock Warren began the infantry attack, his right flank covered by Mackenzie's cavalry, and, at the same time, General Merritt made a lively demonstration against the enemy's right. Although the two leading infantry divisions barely escaped disaster through getting separated, the error was rectified in time, and as the infantry swarmed over the left and rear of the enemy's works, doubling up the Confederate line in confusion, Devin's cavalry division went over the works in front.[3] The hostile artillery was captured and was quickly turned on the demoralized enemy. At the same time Custer was having an obstinate battle on the left with Corse's and Terry's infantry and W. H. F. Lee's cavalry.

---

3. "The dismounted cavalry had assaulted as soon as they heard the infantry fire open. The natty cavalrymen, with their tight-fitting jackets and short carbines, swarmed through the pine thickets and dense undergrowth, looking as if they had been especially built for crawling through knot-holes." (General Horace Porter's *Campaigning with Grant,* in the *Century Magazine.*)

After the first line was carried, the enemy made no serious stand, and the spoils of the battle were six guns, thirteen battle-flags, and nearly 6,000 prisoners. Fearing Lee would escape, Grant ordered a general assault on the enemy's works the next day, and the entrenchments were carried at several points. Merritt on the same day was moving westward, and drove a considerable force of the enemy s cavalry from a point north of Hatcher's Run to Scott's Corners.

During the night of the 2nd, General Lee evacuated Richmond and Petersburg and moved towards Danville.

On the 3rd the cavalry resumed their pursuit, the Fifth Corps in support, and five pieces of artillery and hundreds of prisoners were taken. The enemy's infantry rear guard was overtaken at Deep Creek, where a severe fight took place, and Merritt was directed to await Crook's arrival and that of a division of the Fifth Corps.

As Lee seemed to be heading for Amelia Court House, Crook was ordered on the 4th to push ahead and strike the Danville Railroad, which he did near Jetersville; and the Fifth Corps, following close be hind, entrenched itself at that point.

While at Jetersville, a telegram from Lee's commissary-general to the supply departments at Danville and Lynchburg was intercepted, ordering 3,000,000 rations sent to Burkeville. The telegram was re-transmitted by Sheridan, who determined forthwith to secure the rations for his own army.

On the morning of the 5th General Davies made a reconnaissance towards Payne's Cross-Roads and discovered that Lee's army was attempting to escape in that direction. Davies succeeded in burning nearly 200 of the enemy's wagons, and rejoined the supporting brigades of Smith and Gregg near Flat Creek, eluding a strong force of Confederate infantry, which had been sent out to cut off his retreat.

It became apparent to Sheridan on the following day that the entire mass of Lee's army was attempting to escape. His trains, heavily escorted, were found moving towards Burkeville, and there were other evidences of a general retreat. At this time. Meade's plan of attack was to advance his right flank to Amelia Court House, but, after carrying out this manoeuvre, he found Lee gone, just as Sheridan had predicted, when, on April 4th and 5th, the cavalry leader wished to attack Lee with his cavalry and the Second Army Corps.

Crook was sent against Lee's train on the Deatonsville road, but found them strongly guarded. So Sheridan shifted the cavalry across country, parallel to Lee's line of march, hoping to find a weak point in his column. To prevent the detaching of any of the enemy's forces, the Michigan brigade (Stagg's) of the First Division, with Miller's battery, remained a few miles south of Deatonsville and made a strong demonstration. This gained time for the arrival of the Sixth Army Corps, then marching to join Sheridan.

A favourable opportunity for the attack of the long Confederate column occurred at Sailor's Creek, where Custer, with the Third Cavalry Division, charged the force guarding the trains, routed it, and captured over 300 wagons. While Custer was thus engaged, the Confederates were reinforced by Kershaw's and Custis Lee's infantry divisions under Ewell. The First Cavalry Division was pushed forward by Merritt to Custer s assistance, and as Stagg's brigade of this division moved up on the left of the Third Division it made a brilliant charge, which resulted in the capture of 300 prisoners, and with the arrival of the other brigades the enemy's line was broken. This success, supported by the position of Crook's cavalry division, which had been planted squarely across the enemy s line of march, had the effect of cutting off three of the enemy's infantry divisions; and as the Sixth Corps moved up in the enemy's rear, nearly the entire force was captured. This included General Ewell and 6 of his generals, fifteen guns, thirty-one battle-flags, and from 9,000 to 10,000 prisoners. The battle had also the effect of deflecting Longstreet's corps from its march to wards Danville, and it moved to Farmville, north of Appomattox.

Sheridan at this time wrote to Grant, "If the thing is pressed, I think that Lee will surrender." And President Lincoln telegraphed Grant the laconic message, "Let the thing be pressed."

It was pressed. On the 7th Crook's division was pushed on to Farmville; and Merritt and Mackenzie to Prince Edward's Court House to prevent any movement of the enemy towards Danville.

Crook overtook the rear guard of the enemy's train just across the river at Farmville, and in a sharp fight, by Gregg's brigade, was repulsed.[4]

This action indicated clearly that Lee's objective was Lynchburg. This being the case, Sheridan determined to throw all his cavalry across the enemy's path, and hold him, if possible, until the infantry could arrive.

Accordingly Merritt and Mackenzie were recalled, joining Crook at daylight, April 8th, at Prospect Station, and all the cavalry were hurried on towards Appomattox Depôt, twenty-eight miles away. Custer, having the advance, detached two regiments to cut off four[5] trains of stores destined for Lee's army, which were found a short distance out of Appomattox, and then, turning his attention to the depôt, charged the enemy's advance guard just approaching.

The First Division was soon brought up by Merritt, and, being deployed, dismounted, on the right of the Third, it

---

4. General Gregg was captured, and the command of his brigade devolved upon Colonel S. B. M. Young, Fourth Pennsylvania Cavalry.
5. Sheridan says four trains; Merritt and Custer report three.

crossed the road along which the enemy was attempting to move, and effectually blocked his retreat.

The enemy was driven in this fight, which continued until after dark, towards Appomattox Court House, and twenty-four pieces of artillery, an immense train, and many prisoners fell into the hands of the cavalry.

The day's work of the cavalry was most important. As General Merritt has said: "The enemy's supplies were taken, as it were, out of their mouths. A strong force they knew not how strong was posted along their line of retreat at a point where they did not expect opposition. Night was upon them. Tired, desperate, and starving, they lay at our feet. Their bravest soldiers, their hardiest men gave way when they heard the noise of battle far in the rear, and the night of despair fell with the night of the 8th of April, darkly and terribly, on the Army of Northern Virginia."[6]

During the night of the 8th, urgent efforts were made to hurry up the infantry reinforcements under Ord, and about daylight on the 9th the Twenty-fourth and Fifth Corps and one division of the Twenty-fifth Corps arrived at Appomattox Depôt. Soon after, the movement which General Lee had agreed upon during the night — namely, that Gordon should break through the Federal cavalry — was begun under stress of over whelming numbers. Merritt's cavalry division was directed to fall back to the right and rear, resisting; and Crook and Mackenzie on the left of the line were instructed to hold their ground as long as possible, without sacrificing their men.

As the enemy caught sight of the long lines of Ord's infantry, he realized that further resistance was useless, and discontinued the attack. About this time Merritt was ordered to move against the enemy's left, and, in spite of a heavy artillery fire, the First and Third Cavalry Divisions

6. Report of April 20, 1865.

secured possession of high ground within half a mile of the Court House.

Preparations were being made to attack the exposed Confederate flank with Custer's and Devin's divisions, when a flag of truce called for a suspension of hostilities, and, so far as the cavalry of the Army of the Potomac was concerned, the War of the Rebellion was practically over.

The cavalry was marched to Petersburg, and on April 24th was moved southward with a view to aiding General Sherman's army. But upon reaching South Boston, on the Dan River, Sheridan received word of General Johnston's surrender, and the cavalry retraced its steps to Petersburg, from whence, by easy stages, it marched to Washington. On May 23rd, amid the cheers of thousands, it took part in "The Grand Review," as fine a body of cavalry as the world has ever seen.

CHAPTER 23
Civil War Cavalry: an Overview

The development of the cavalry of the Army of the Potomac was perhaps the most wonderful object lesson of the entire war.

Given a mass of citizen-soldiers, undisciplined, undrilled, many of them ignorant of arms and of horses, men from the factory and men from the counting-house, engineers off the railroad and professors from colleges; to take these and in four years to mould them into that magnificent body of horsemen which constituted Sheridan's command at Appomattox is something that is distinctively a production of the active, physical, and mental energy, the intelligence, the resources, and, above all, the patriotism, of the American nation.

It would be absurd to draw comparisons between the courage of the soldiers of Stuart and those of Pleasanton; between those of Fitzhugh Lee and those of Sheridan. They were all Americans, and, whether born beneath Southern suns or Northern stars, possessed equally American pluck, endurance, and bravery.

But the Southern soldiers were natural horsemen, and, under the wise patronage of General Lee and the dashing leadership of Stuart, the Confederate cavalry from the beginning exhibited that independence of action, whether mounted or dismounted, which made them so formidable to the Federal Army. At the beginning of the Gettysburg campaign, no finer type of cavalry could be found anywhere than the cavalry of Stuart; and the stimulus of such a standard of excellence contributed not a little towards producing a Federal cavalry which could successfully cope with their adversaries. But the greatest influence in making the National Cavalry was its concentration under one competent commander.

That it did so is a matter of history, and the superiority arose from a number of causes. The first two years of the war, though years of inferiority for the Federal cavalry, were filled with valuable lessons, far-reaching in their effects. The use of arms and the care of horses natural from birth to the Southerner was hammered into the daily life of the Northerner with a persistent thoroughness which was a remarkable characteristic of his nature; and this constant attention to the minutiae of a cavalryman's life had its ultimate effect in producing men equally skillful with sabre, pistol, and carbine. The sabre was considered the first weapon of the Union cavalry, but in the use of the repeating carbine it showed that its effective fire-action was not lessened by its effective shock- action. The fact, too, that in the Army of Northern Virginia each trooper was required to furnish his horse, undoubtedly had its effect upon the degeneracy of the Confederate cavalry. Other causes the loss of Stuart and the rise of Sheridan, as well as the gradual draining of the resources of the Confederacy, men and materials, all these contributed to the final result.

It is best now to think of the cavalry of both great armies as exemplifying to the entire world all that was greatest and best in the organization, equipment, and use of the mounted arm. To be sure, a certain class of European critics continue, with almost wilful persistence, to misrepresent the true character of our cavalry and its use during the greatest of modern wars. That our cavalry cast aside the moss-grown traditions of European tacticians, rejecting all that was obsolete, retaining all that was best, and developing that which their sound common sense indicated would add to their fighting efficiency, is to their lasting credit. They created a new role for the mounted army and proved to their own satisfaction, as Kilpatrick has said, that "cavalry can fight anywhere, except at sea."

Laying aside the question of cavalry raids, those independent, self-sustaining operations which were a distinct product of the War of the Rebellion, examples are not wanting of the most glorious use of the cavalry, both mounted and dismounted, throughout the war.

Side by side with the charge of the German cavalry at Mars-la-Tour, we can place the effective charge of the Eighth Pennsylvania Cavalry under Huey, at Chancellorsville. For the charge of the English Light Brigade at Balaclava, we can name that of the lamented Farnsworth upon the Confederate right flank at Gettysburg. With the charge of the French cuirassiers at Sedan, we can class the devoted charge of the First and Fifth United States Cavalry at Gaines Mill, or that of the Sixth United States and Sixth Pennsylvania upon the Confederate artillery at Brandy Station.

Was there ever a finer or more effective cavalry charge against infantry than that of Merritt's division upon the Confederate left flank at Opequon? Was there ever a grander cavalry battle than that of Beverly Ford, or the desperate fight of Gregg's division upon the right flank at Gettysburg?

And was ever before seen the spectacle of these same cavalry troops, dismounted, holding in check long lines of the enemy's infantry, as did the troopers of the gallant Buford at Gettysburg, or the cavalry under the peerless Sheridan at Dinwiddie Court House? Does the world believe that cavalry was none the less true cavalry when, like Gamble's brigade at Upperville, it dismounted behind stone walls, in order to check a cavalry charge with a withering fire from their carbines; or, as did Devin's division at Five Forks, carrying the enemy's works, side by side with their comrades of the infantry?

No; it will be the proud boast of the cavalry of the Army of the Potomac that it created where others had been content to follow; that it shattered the traditions of the Old World and builded them anew. Its deeds are too indelibly written upon the pages of history to ever be effaced; and, though for a time misunderstood, misused, and misrepresented, it at last vindicated itself in a way which the cavalry of the future will do well to emulate.

Sources

The writer has depended for his statements almost entirely upon that best of all authorities the official records of the Union and Confederate armies but a list of the principal supplementary works consulted is appended.

Official Records of the War of the Rebellion.

History of the United States Cavalry (Brackett).

The Second Dragoons (Rodenbough).

History of the First Maine Cavalry (Tobie).

History of the First New York (Lincoln) Cavalry (Stevenson).

Annals of the Sixth Pennsylvania Cavalry (Gracey).

Battles and Leaders of the Civil War (The Century Co.).

The Shenandoah Valley in 1864 (Post).

Cavalry in the Gettysburg Campaign (Davis).

Sheridan's Memoirs.

The Civil War (Abbott).

History of the Civil War (Comte de Paris).

History of the United States (Eliot).

Organization and Tactics (Wagner).

Operations of War (Hamley).

Journal of the U. S. Cavalry Association.

Appendices

The following pages of the Appendix are almost entirely statistical, and are merely added for reference in order to make the entire history of the cavalry as complete as possible in itself:

APPENDIX 1.

Copy of the letter from the Secretary of War, authorizing the raising of the First Regiment of volunteer cavalry:*

War Department, Washington, May 1, 1861.

To the Governors of the Several States, and All Whom It may Concern:

I have authorized Colonel Carl Schurz to raise and organize a volunteer regiment of cavalry. For the purpose of rendering it as efficient as possible, he is instructed to enlist principally such men as have served in the same arm before. The Government will provide the regiment with arms, but cannot provide the horses and equipments. For these necessaries we rely upon the patriotism of the States and the citizens, and for this purpose I take the liberty of requesting you to afford Colonel Schurz your aid in the execution of this plan.

(Signed) SIMON CAMERON,
Secretary of War.

APPENDIX 2.

Organization of the cavalry, Army of the Potomac, October 15, 1861:

---

*By authority of this letter, the First Regiment of New York (Lincoln) Cavalry was organized.

Brigadier-General Stoneman's cavalry command:—
    Fifth United States Cavalry.
    Fourth Pennsylvania Cavalry.
    Oneida Cavalry (one company).
    Eleventh Pennsylvania Cavalry (Harlan's).
    Barker's Illinois Cavalry (one company).
Attached to City Guard—4th U. S. Cavalry, Cos. A and E.
Attached to Banks' Division—3d Regiment, New York Cavalry (four companies).
Attached to McDowell's Division—2d New York Cavalry (Harris Light).
Attached to Heintzelman's Division—1st New Jersey Cavalry.
Attached to Porter's Division—3d Pennsylvania Cavalry, 8th Pennsylvania Cavalry.
Attached to Franklin's Division—1st New York Cavalry.
Attached to Stone's Division—3d New York Cavalry (six companies).
Attached to McCall's Division—1st Pennsylvania Cavalry.
Attached to Hooker's Division—3d Indiana Cavalry (eight companies).
Attached to Blenker's Brigade—4th New York Cavalry (Mounted Rifles).
Attached to Dix's Division—(Baltimore) one company of Pennsylvania Cavalry.

APPENDIX 3.

Organization of the cavalry, Army of the Potomac, during the operations before Richmond, June 25 to July 2, 1862:

Attached to Second Army Corps—6th New York Cavalry, Cos. D, F, H, and K.
Attached to Third Army Corps—3d Pennsylvania Cavalry.
Attached to Fourth Army Corps—8th Pennsylvania Cavalry.
Attached to Fifth Army Corps—8th Illinois Cavalry.
Attached to Third Division, Fifth Army Corps—4th Pennsylvania Cavalry.
Attached to Second Division, Sixth Army Corps—5th Pennsylvania Cavalry. Cos. I and K.

Attached to Sixth Army Corps—1st New York Cavalry (unattached).

Brigadier-General Philip St. George Cooke.

6th Pennsylvania Cavalry.	6th U. S. Cavalry.
1st U. S. Cavalry, Cos. A, C, F, and H.	5th U. S. Cavalry, Cos. A, D, F, H, and I.

Cavalry Troops at General Headquarters—McClellan Dragoons, Oneida (New York) Cavalry, 2d U. S. Cavalry, 4th U. S. Cavalry, Cos. A and E.

APPENDIX 4.

Organization of the Union cavalry at the battle of Cedar Mountain, Va., August 9, 1862:

Escort at General Headquarters—1st Ohio Cavalry, Cos. A and C.

Escort at Headquarters, Second Army Corps—1st Michigan Cavalry (detachment), 5th New York Cavalry (detachment), 1st West Virginia Cavalry (detachment).

Cavalry Brigade.

Brigadier-General George D. Bayard.

1st Maine Cavalry.	1st New Jersey Cavalry.
1st Pennsylvania Cavalry.	1st Rhode Island Cavalry.

APPENDIX 5.

Organization of the cavalry of the Army of Virginia (Pope's) during the operations August 16 to September 2, 1862, inclusive:

Headquarters escort—1st Ohio Cavalry, Cos. A and C.

Escort at Headquarters First Army Corps—1st Indiana Cavalry, Cos. I and K.

Attached to First Army Corps—3d West Virginia Cavalry, Co. C.

Attached to Independent Brigade—1st West Virginia Cavalry, Cos. C, E, and L.

Cavalry Brigade of the First Army Corps.
Colonel John Beardsley.

1st Connecticut Battalion.	9th New York Cavalry.
1st Maryland Cavalry.	6th Ohio Cavalry.
4th New York Cavalry.	

Cavalry Brigade of the Second Army Corps.
Brigadier-General John Buford.

1st Michigan Cavalry.	1st Vermont Cavalry.
5th New York Cavalry.	1st West Virginia Cavalry.

Cavalry Brigade of the Third Army Corps.
Brigadier-General George D. Bayard.

1st Maine Cavalry.	1st Pennsylvania Cavalry.
2d New York Cavalry.	1st Rhode Island Cavalry.
1st New Jersey.	

Unattached—3d Indiana Cavalry (detachment).

APPENDIX 6.

Organization of cavalry, Army of the Potomac, September 14, 17, 1862 (South Mountain and Antietam):

Escort at General Headquarters—Independent Company, Oneida (New York) Cavalry; 4th U. S. Cavalry, Cos. A and E.

Attached to Provost Guard—2d U. S. Cavalry, Cos. E, F, H, K.

Quartermaster's Guard—1st U. S. Cavalry, Cos. B, C, H, I.

Escort Headquarters First Army Corps—2d New York Cavalry, Cos. A, B, I, K.

Escort to Second Army Corps—6th New York Cavalry, Cos. D and K.

Escort to Headquarters Fifth Army Corps—1st Maine Cavalry (detachment).

Escort to Headquarters Sixth Army Corps—6th Pennsylvania Cavalry, Ccs. B and G.
Escort to Headquarters Ninth Army Corps—1st Maine Cavalry, Co. G.
Escort to Headquarters Twelfth Army Corps—1st Michigan Cavalry, Co. L.

Cavalry Division.

Brigadier-General Alfred Pleasanton, U. S. Army.

1st Brigade—Major Charles Whiting.

5th U. S. Cavalry.
6th U. S. Cavalry.

2d Brigade—Colonel John F. Farnsworth.

8th Illinois Cavalry.
3d Indiana Cavalry.
1st Massachusetts Cavalry.
8th Pennsylvania Cavalry.

3d Brigade—Col. Richard H. Rush.

4th Pennsylvania Cavalry.
6th Pennsylvania Cavalry.

4th Brigade—Col. Andrew T. McReynolds.

1st New York Cavalry.
12th Pennsylvania Cavalry.

5th Brigade—Colonel Benj. F. Davis.

8th New York Cavalry.
3d Pennsylvania Cavalry.

Unattached.

1st Maine Cavalry.
15th Pennsylvania Cavalry (detachment).

Artillery (attached to 2d and 3d Brigades).

2d U. S. Artillery, Batteries A, B, L, M.
3d U. S. Artillery, Batteries C, G.

APPENDIX 7.

Report of officers, enlisted men, and horses in the cavalry and light artillery, Army of the Potomac, November 1, 1862:

| | Officers | Men. | TRANSPORTATION. | | | HORSES. | | No. of Public Animals. |
			Horses.	Mules.	Army Wagons.	Cavalry.	Artillery.	
Cavalry and Light Artillery.........	396	7,995	752	541	276	7,063	630	8,986

APPENDIX 8.

Organization of the cavalry, Army of the Potomac, at the battle of Fredericksburg, Va., December 11-15, 1862:

Escort at General Headquarters—Oneida (New York) Cavalry. 1st U. S. Cavalry (detachment), 4th U. S. Cavalry, Cos. A and E.

Attached to Provost Guard—McClellan (Illinois) Dragoons, Cos. A and B; 2d U. S. Cavalry.

Escort at Headquarters Ninth Army Corps—6th New York Cavalry, Cos. B and C.

Escort at Headquarters First Army Corps—1st Maine Cavalry, Co. L.

Escort at Headquarters Sixth Army Corps—10th New York Cavalry, Co. L; 6th Pennsylvania Cavalry, Cos. I and K.

Cavalry Division Attached to Right Grand Division.

Brigadier-General Alfred Pleasanton.

1st Brigade—Brig.-Gen. John F. Farnsworth.
8th Illinois Cavalry.
3d Indiana Cavalry.
8th New York Cavalry.
Artillery—2d U. S. Battery M.

2d Brigade—(1) Colonel David McM. Gregg; (2) Colonel Thomas C. Devin.
6th New York Cavalry.
8th Pennsylvania Cavalry.
6th U. S. Cavalry.

Cavalry Brigade Attached to Center Grand Division.

Brigadier-General William W. Averell.

1st Massachusetts Cavalry. 4th Pennsylvania Cavalry.
3d Pennsylvania Cavalry. 5th U. S. Cavalry.
Artillery—2d U. S., Batteries B and L.

Cavalry Brigade Attached to Left Grand Division.

(1) Brigadier-General George D. Bayard; (2) Colonel David McM. Gregg.

1st Maine Cavalry. District of Columbia, Inde-
2d New York Cavalry. pendent Co.
1st Pennsylvania Cavalry. 1st New Jersey Cavalry.
10th New York Cavalry.
Artillery—3d U. S., Battery C.

APPENDIX 9.

Organization of the cavalry, Army of the Potomac, May 1-6, 1863 (Chancellorsville Campaign):

Attached to the command of Provost-Marshal-General—6th Pennsylvania Cavalry, Detachment of Regular Cavalry.
Guards and Orderlies—Oneida (New York) Cavalry.
Escort Headquarters First Army Corps—1st Maine Cavalry, Co. L.
Escort Second Army Corps—6th New York, Cos. D and K.
Escort Headquarters Sixth Army Corps—1st New Jersey Cavalry, 1st Pennsylvania Cavalry.
Escort Headquarters Eleventh Army Corps—1st Indiana, Cos. I and K.

CAVALRY CORPS.[*]

Brigadier-General George Stoneman.

First Division.

Brigadier-General Alfred Pleasanton.

1st Brigade—Colonel Benj. F. Davis.	2d Brigade—Colonel Thos. C. Devin.
8th Illinois Cavalry.	1st Michigan Cavalry.
3d Indiana Cavalry.	6th New York Cavalry.
8th New York Cavalry.	8th Pennsylvania Cavalry.
9th New York Cavalry.	17th Pennsylvania Cavalry.

Artillery—New York Light, 6th Battery.

Second Division.

Brigadier-General William W. Averell.

1st Brigade—Col. Horace B. Sargent.	2d Brigade—Colonel John B. McIntosh.
1st Massachusetts Cavalry.	3d Pennsylvania Cavalry.
4th New York Cavalry.	4th Pennsylvania Cavalry.
6th Ohio Cavalry.	16th Pennsylvania Cavalry.
1st Rhode Island Cavalry.	

Artillery—2d United States, Battery A.

Third Division.

Brigadier-General David McM. Gregg.

1st Brigade—Colonel Judson Kilpatrick.	2d Brigade—Colonel Percy Wyndham.
1st Maine Cavalry.	12th Illinois Cavalry.
2d New York Cavalry.	1st Maryland Cavalry.
10th New York Cavalry.	1st New Jersey Cavalry.
	1st Pennsylvania Cavalry.

Regular Reserve Cavalry Brigade.

Brigadier-General John Buford.

6th Pennsylvania Cavalry.	5th U. S. Cavalry.
1st U. S. Cavalry.	6th U. S. Cavalry.
2d U. S. Cavalry.	

---

[*]The Second and Third Divisions, First Brigade, First Division, and the Reserve Brigade, with Robertson's and Tidball's batteries were on the "Stoneman Raid," April 29th to May 2d.

Artillery.

Captain Jas. M. Robertson.

Second United States, Batteries B and M.   Fourth United States, Battery E.

APPENDIX 10.

Organization of the cavalry, Army of the Potomac, at the battle of Gettysburg, July 1-3, 1863:

Attached to the command of the Provost-Marshal-General—2d Pennsylvania Cavalry, 6th Pennsylvania Cavalry, Regular Cavalry (detachments from 1st, 2d, 5th, and 6th Regiments).

Guards and Orderlies—Oneida (New York) Cavalry.

Escort Headquarters First Army Corps—1st Maine Cavalry, Co. L.

Escort Headquarters Second Army Corps—6th New York Cavalry, Cos. D and K.

Escort Headquarters Fifth Army Corps—17th Pennsylvania Cavalry, Cos. D and K.

Escort Headquarters Sixth Army Corps—1st New Jersey Cavalry, Co. L: 1st Pennsylvania Cavalry, Co. H.

Escort Headquarters Eleventh Army Corps—1st Indiana Cavalry, Cos. I and K.

CAVALRY CORPS.

Major-General Alfred Pleasanton.

First Division.

Brigadier-General John Buford.

1st Brigade—Colonel William Gamble.

8th Illinois Cavalry.
12th Illinois Cavalry (4 Cos.).
3d Indiana Cavalry (6 Cos.).
8th New York Cavalry.

2d Brigade—Colonel Thos. C. Devin.

6th New York Cavalry.
9th New York Cavalry.
17th Pennsylvania Cavalry.
3d West Virginia Cavalry (2 Cos.).

Reserve Brigade—Brig.-Gen. Wesley Merritt.
6th Pennsylvania Cavalry.
1st U. S. Cavalry.
2d U. S. Cavalry.
5th U. S. Cavalry.
6th U. S. Cavalry.

Second Division.
Brigadier-General David McM. Gregg.
Headquarters Guard—1st Ohio Cavalry, Co. A.

1st Brigade—Colonel John B. McIntosh.

1st Maryland Cavalry (11 Cos.).
Purnell (Md.) Legion.
1st Massachusetts Cavalry.*
1st New Jersey Cavalry.
1st Pennsylvania Cavalry.
3d Pennsylvania Cavalry.
3d Pennsylvania Heavy Artillery (section Bat. H).†

2d Brigade‡—Colonel Pennock Huey.

2d New York Cavalry.
4th New York Cavalry.
6th Ohio Cavalry (10 Cos.).
8th Pennsylvania Cavalry.

3d Brigade—Colonel J. Irvin Gregg.

1st Maine Cavalry (10 Cos.).
10th New York Cavalry.
4th Pennsylvania Cavalry.
16th Pennsylvania Cavalry.

Third Division.
Brigadier-General Judson Kilpatrick.
Headquarters Guard—1st Ohio Cavalry, Co. C.

1st Brigade—(1) Brig.-Gen. E. J. Farnsworth; (2) Col. Nath'l P. Richmond.

5th New York Cavalry.
18th Pennsylvania Cavalry.
1st Vermont Cavalry.
1st West Virginia Cavalry (10 Cos.).

2d Brigade—Brig.-Gen. Geo. A. Custer.

1st Michigan Cavalry.
5th Michigan Cavalry.
6th Michigan Cavalry.
7th Michigan Cavalry.

---

*Served with Sixth Army Corps and on the right flank.

†Serving as light artillery.

‡At Westminster, and not engaged in battle.

154

Horse Artillery.

1st Brigade—Capt. James C. Robertson.

9th Michigan Battery.
6th New York Battery.
2d U. S., Batteries B, L, M.
4th U. S., Battery E.

2d Brigade—Captain John C. Tidball.

1st U. S., Batteries E, G, K.
2d U. S., Battery A.
3d U. S., Battery C.*

APPENDIX 11.

Field report of the Cavalry Corps, Army of the Potomac, June 28, 1863 (preceding the battle of Gettysburg):

	Officers.	Enlisted Men.	Horses of Officers.	Horses of Enlisted Men.	Officers Sick.	Enlisted Men Sick.	Horses Serviceable.	Horses Unserviceable.
Corps Headquarters....	20	300	60	275	....	.....	355	.....
1st Division............	179	4,019	.....	....	3	113	4,570	590
2d Division	266	4,347	.....	....	7	156	4,534	834
Stahel's Division.......	231	3,291	.....	....	8	331	†......	†.....
Brigade Horse Artillery	7	484	.....	....	2	20	736	......
Total	703	12,441	60	275	20	620	10,195	1,424

†Not reported.

APPENDIX 12.

Organization of the cavalry operating against Richmond, May 5, 1864 (Army of the Potomac):

Attached to Provost Guard—1st Massachusetts Cavalry, Cos. C and D.

Guards and Orderlies—Independent Company, Oneida (New York) Cavalry.

*With Huey's cavalry brigade, and not engaged in battle.

Escort to Headquarters Second Army Corps—1st Vermont Cavalry, Co. M.

Escort to Headquarters Sixth Army Corps—8th Pennsylvania Cavalry, Co A.

Attached to Ninth Army Corps—3d New Jersey Cavalry, 22d New York Cavalry, 2d Ohio Cavalry, 13th Pennsylvania Cavalry.

Attached to Provisional Brigade—24th New York Cavalry (dismounted).

CAVALRY CORPS.

General Philip H. Sheridan.

First Division.

Brig.-General Alfred T. A. Torbert, Escort 6th U. S. Cavalry.

1st Brigade—Brig.-Gen. Geo. A. Custer.

1st Michigan Cavalry.
5th Michigan Cavalry.
6th Michigan Cavalry.
7th Michigan Cavalry.

2d Brigade—Colonel Thos. C. Devin.

4th New York Cavalry.
6th New York Cavalry.
9th New York Cavalry.
17th Pennsylvania Cavalry.

Reserve Brigade—Brig.-Gen. Wesley Merritt.

19th New York Cavalry (1st Dragoons).
6th Pennsylvania Cavalry.
1st United States Cavalry.
2d United States Cavalry.
5th United States Cavalry.

Second Division.

Brigadier-General David McM. Gregg.

1st Brigade—Brig.-Gen. H. E. Davies, Jr.

1st Massachusetts Cavalry.
1st New Jersey Cavalry.
6th Ohio Cavalry.
1st Pennsylvania Cavalry.

2d Brigade—Colonel J. Irvin Gregg.

1st Maine Cavalry.
10th New York Cavalry.
2d Pennsylvania Cavalry.
4th Pennsylvania Cavalry.
8th Pennsylvania Cavalry.
16th Pennsylvania Cavalry.

Third Division.

Brigadier-General James H. Wilson.

Escort—8th Illinois Cavalry (detachment).

1st Brigade—Colonel Timothy M. Bryan, Jr.; Col. J. B. McIntosh (assigned May 5th).
1st Connecticut Cavalry.
2d New York Cavalry.
5th New York Cavalry.
18th Pennsylvania Cavalry.

2d Brigade—Col. George H. Chapman.
3d Indiana Cavalry.
8th New York Cavalry.
1st Vermont Cavalry.

Cavalry of the Army of the James.

Unattached—1st Battalion, 4th Massachusetts Cavalry.

Cavalry Division—Brigadier-General August V. Kautz.

1st Brigade—Colonel Simon H. Mix.
1st District Columbia Cavalry.
3d New York Cavalry.

2d Brigade—Colonel Samuel P. Spear.
5th Pennsylvania Cavalry.
11th Pennsylvania Cavalry.

Unattached.
1st New York Mounted Rifles.
1st U. S. Colored Cavalry.
2d. U. S. Cavalry.

APPENDIX 13.

Organization of the cavalry of the Army of the Potomac in the operations against Richmond, August 31, 1864:

Attached to Provost Guard—1st Indiana Cavalry, Co. K; 1st Massachusetts Cavalry, Cos. C and D; 3d Pennsylvania Cavalry, Cos. A, B, and M.
Guards and Orderlies—Independent Company, Oneida (New York) Cavalry.

Escort at Headquarters Ninth Army Corps—3d New Jersey Cavalry (detachment).

CAVALRY.

Second Division.

Brigadier-General David McM. Gregg.

1st Brigade—Colonel William Stedman.

1st Massachusetts Cavalry.
1st New Jersey Cavalry.
10th New York Cavalry.
6th Ohio Cavalry.
1st Pennsylvania Cavalry.

2d Brigade—Colonel Charles H. Smith.

1st Maine Cavalry.
2d Pennsylvania Cavalry.
4th Pennsylvania Cavalry.
8th Pennsylvania Cavalry.
13th Pennsylvania Cavalry.
16th Pennsylvania Cavalry.

Recapitulation.

Abstract from tri-monthly returns showing present for duty equipment or effective strength of the armies operating against Richmond, under General U. S. Grant, August 31 to December 31, 1864.

ARM.	Aug. 31st.	Sept. 30th.	Oct. 31st.	Nov. 30th.	Dec 31st.
Infantry	45,963	66,818	76,637	77,387	92,141
Cavalry	6,358	7,122	6,295	8,698	10,059
Artillery	7,846	10,182	8,011	10,294	9,719
Aggregate	60,167	84,122	90,943	96,379	111,919

APPENDIX 14.

Effective force of the First and Third Cavalry Divisions, Army of the Shenandoah, February 28, 1865. Major-General Wesley Merritt, chief-of-cavalry:

	Officers.	Men.	Total.
First Cavalry Division (Devin's).....	260	4,787	5,047
One Section, Companies C and E, 4th U. S. Artillery	2	52	54
Third Cavalry Division (Custer's).....	240	4,600	4,840
One Section, Company M, 2d U. S. Artillery...... ...	1	45	46
Total....	503	9,484	9,987

APPENDIX 15.

Abstract from the returns of the cavalry commanded by Major-General Philip H. Sheridan, U. S. A., for the month of March, 1865:

COMMAND.	Present for Duty.		Aggregate Pres'nt	Aggregate Pres'nt and Absent.	Pieces of Artillery.	
	Officers	Men.			Heavy.	Field.
1st Division (Devin).						
General Headquarters...... ...	5	....	5	5	......	......
1st Brigade (Stagg).............	48	956	1,344	4,801	......	......
2d Brigade (Fitzhugh).........	82	1,168	1,495	5,417	......	......
Reserve Brigade (Gibbs)	20	659	825	3,365	......	......
Artillery (Miller).............	2	47	50	157	......	2
Total............	166	2,830	3,719	13,745	......	2
3d Division (Custer).						
General Headquarters.........	3	....	3	3	....	......
1st Brigade (Pennington)......	81	1,294	1,570	4,747	....	......
2d Brigade (Wells)..	70	1,725	1,959	3,884	......	......
3d Brigade (Capehart)	55	1,336	1,725	3,196	....	......
Total.	209	4,355	5,257	11,830	....	......
Grand Total Army of Shenandoah	375	7,185	8,976	25,575	......	2

COMMAND.	Present for Duty.		Aggregate Present	Aggregate Pres'nt and Absent.	Pieces of Artillery.	
	Officers	Men.			Heavy.	Field.
ARMY OF POTOMAC.						
2d Division (Crook).						
General Headquarters	5	.....	5	5	....	....
1st Brigade (Davies).	91	2,147	2,776	3,950	....	.....
2d Brigade (Gregg).	66	1,752	3,366	4,651	....	.....
3d Brigade (Smith)..	48	1,516	2,270	4,104	......	....
Artillery..................	6	235	265	338	......	8
Total..	216	5,656	8,682	13,048	.....	8
Grand Total...................	591	12,835	17,658	38,623	......	10

APPENDIX 16.

Organization of the Union Cavalry in the Appomattox campaign, March 29 to April 9, 1865:

Escort to General Grant's Headquarters—5th U. S. Cavalry, Cos. B, F, and K.

Attached to Provost Guard of the Army of the Potomac—1st Indiana Cavalry, Co. K; 1st Massachusetts Cavalry, Cos. C and D; 3d Pennsylvania Cavalry.

Quartermaster's Guard—Independent Company, Oneida (New York) Cavalry.

Escort Headquarters Fifth Army Corps—4th Pennsylvania Cavalry, Co. C.

Escort Headquarters Sixth Army Corps—21st Pennsylvania Cavalry, Co. E.

Attached to Ninth Army Corps—2d Pennsylvania Cavalry.

Attached to Independent Brigade—1st Massachusetts Cavalry (8 companies).

CAVALRY.

Major-General Philip H. Sheridan.

Army of the Shenandoah—Brevet Brig.-General Wesley Merritt.

First Division.

Brigadier-General Thomas C. Devin.

1st Brigade—Colonel Peter Stagg.

1st Michigan Cavalry.
5th Michigan Cavalry.
6th Michigan Cavalry.
7th Michigan Cavalry.

2d Brigade—Colonel Chas. L. Fitzhugh.

6th New York Cavalry.
9th New York Cavalry.
19th New York Cavalry.
17th Pennsylvania Cav.l y
20th Pennsylvania Cavaliy.

Reserve Brigade—Brig.-Gen. Alfred Gibbs.

2d Massachusetts Cavaliy.
1st United States Cavalry.
6th United States Cavalry.
6th Pennsylvania Cavalry (6 companies).
5th United States Cavalry.

Third Division.

Brigadier-General George A. Custer.

1st Brigade—Colonel A. C. M. Pennington.

1st Connecticut Cavalry.
3d New Jersey Cavalry.
2d New York Cavalry.
2d Ohio Cavalry.

2d Brigade—Colonel William Wells.

8th New York Cavalry.
15th New York Cavalry.
1st Vermont Cavalry.

3d Brigade—Col. Henry Capehart.

1st New York (Lincoln) Cavalry.
1st West Virginia Cavalry.
2d West Virginia Cavalry.
3d West Virginia Cavalry.

Second Division.

(Army of the Potomac)—Major-General George Crook.

1st Brigade—Brig.-Gen. Henry E. Davies, Jr.

1st New Jersey Cavalry.
10th New York Cavalry.
24th New York Cavalry.
1st Pennsylvania Cavalry (5 Cos.).
2d U. S. Artillery, Battery A.

2d Brigade—Brvt. Brig.-Gen. J. Irvin Gregg; Colonel Samuel B. M. Young.

4th Pennsylvania Cavalry.
8th Pennsylvania Cavalry.
16th Pennsylvania Cavalry.
21st Pennsylvania Cavalry.
1st U. S. Artillery, Batteries H and I.

3d Brigade—Brevet Brig.-Gen. Chas. B. Smith.

1st Maine Cavalry.
2d New York Mounted Rifles.
6th Ohio Cavalry.
13th Ohio Cavalry.

Cavalry of the Army of the James.

Unattached—4th Massachusetts Cavalry, Cos. I, L, and M; 5th Massachusetts Cavalry (colored); 7th New York Cavalry (1st Mounted Rifles).

Attached to Separate Brigade—20th New York Cavalry, Cos. D and F; 1st United States Colored Cavalry, Cos. B and I.

Headquarters Guard Twenty-fourth Army Corps—4th Massachusetts Cavalry, Cos. F and K.

Provost Guard of the Twenty-fifth Army Corps—4th Massachusetts Cavalry, Cos. E and H.

Attached—2d United States Colored Cavalry.

Cavalry Division.

Brigadier-General Ranald S. Mackenzie.

1st Brigade—Col. Robert M. West.

20th New York Cavalry.
5th Pennsylvania Cavalry.

2d Brigade—Colonel Samuel P. Spear.

1st District of Columbia (battalion).
1st Maryland Cavalry.
11th Pennsylvania Cavalry.

162

LEONAUR

ALSO FROM LEONAUR
AVAILABLE IN SOFTCOVER OR HARDCOVER WITH DUST JACKET

THE JENA CAMPAIGN: 1806 *by F. N. Maude*—The Twin Battles of Jena & Auerstadt Between Napoleon's French and the Prussian Army.

PRIVATE O'NEIL *by Charles O'Neil*—The recollections of an Irish Rogue of H. M. 28th Regt.—The Slashers— during the Peninsula & Waterloo campaigns of the Napoleonic wars.

ROYAL HIGHLANDER by *James Anton*—A soldier of H.M 42nd (Royal) Highlanders during the Peninsular, South of France & Waterloo Campaigns of the Napoleonic Wars.

CAPTAIN BLAZE *by Elzéar Blaze*—Elzéar Blaze recounts his life and experiences in Napoleon's army in a well written, articulate and companionable style.

LEJEUNE VOLUME 1 by *Louis-François Lejeune*—The Napoleonic Wars through the Experiences of an Officer on Berthier's Staff.

LEJEUNE VOLUME 2 by *Louis-François Lejeune*—The Napoleonic Wars through the Experiences of an Officer on Berthier's Staff.

FUSILIER COOPER *by John S. Cooper*—Experiences in the 7th (Royal) Fusiliers During the Peninsular Campaign of the Napoleonic Wars and the American Campaign to New Orleans.

CAPTAIN COIGNET *by Jean-Roch Coignet*—A Soldier of Napoleon's Imperial Guard from the Italian Campaign to Russia and Waterloo.

FIGHTING NAPOLEON'S EMPIRE by *Joseph Anderson*—The Campaigns of a British Infantryman in Italy, Egypt, the Peninsular & the West Indies During the Napoleonic Wars.

CHASSEUR BARRES by *Jean-Baptiste Barres*—The experiences of a French Infantryman of the Imperial Guard at Austerlitz, Jena, Eylau, Friedland, in the Peninsular, Lutzen, Bautzen, Zinnwald and Hanau during the Napoleonic Wars.

MARINES TO 95TH (RIFLES) by *Thomas Fernyhough*—The military experiences of Robert Fernyhough during the Napoleonic Wars.

HUSSAR ROCCA by *Albert Jean Michel de Rocca*—A French cavalry officer's experiences of the Napoleonic Wars and his views on the Peninsular Campaigns against the Spanish, British And Guerilla Armies.

SERGEANT BOURGOGNE by *Adrien Bourgogne*—With Napoleon's Imperial Guard in the Russian Campaign and on the Retreat from Moscow 1812 - 13.